Ten Steps TO A Federal Job®

Jobseeker's Guide

8th Edition

SALVAGE

By Kathryn Troutman
with Paulina Chen

Ten Steps to a Federal Job®
for Military and Spouses

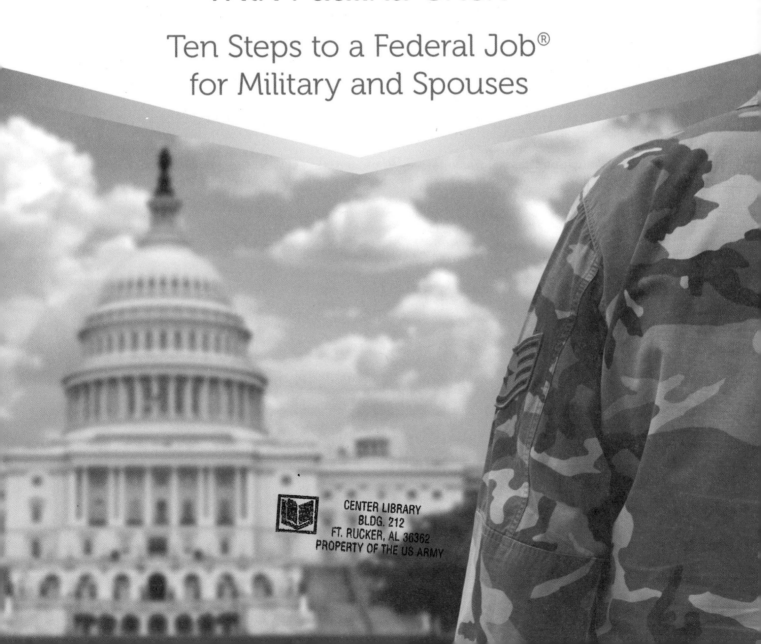

The Resume Place, Inc.
Federal Career Publishers

P.O. Box 21275, Catonsville, MD 21228
Phone: 888-480-8265
www.resume-place.com
Email: govtraining@resume-place.com

Printed in the United States of America
Jobseeker's Guide, 8th Edition: ISBN-13: 978-0-9861421-6-1 | ISBN-10: 986142166
Updated February 2017
Copyright © 2002, 2006, 2009, 2010, 2012, 2013, 2014, 2015, 2016, and 2017 by Kathryn Troutman

Certified Federal Career Coach®, Certified Federal Job Search Trainer®, The Resume Place®, and Ten Steps to a Federal Job® are trademarks of The Resume Place, Inc.

We have been careful to provide accurate federal job search information in this book, but it is possible that errors and omissions may have been introduced.

Attention Transition Counselors, Veterans' Representatives, Workforce Counselors, Career Counselors: The *Jobseeker's Guide* is a training program "handout" to support the Ten Steps to a Federal Job® workshops and PowerPoint program, which is taught at military bases, universities, one-stops, and DoD agencies worldwide. To be licensed to teach the Ten Steps to a Federal Job® curriculum as a Certified Federal Job Search Trainer® or Certified Federal Career Coach®, go to www.resume-place.com for information on our train-the-trainer program. Since the program was developed in 2002, more than 2,000 have been licensed to teach Ten Steps to a Federal Job® with this guide as the handout.

AUTHOR'S NOTES: Sample resumes are real but fictionalized. All federal applicants have given permission for their resumes to be used as samples for this publication. Privacy policy is strictly enforced.

PUBLICATION TEAM
Cover and Interior Page Design: Brian Moore
Developmental Editing, Interior Page Layout, Introduction, Negotiations, Federal Hiring Charts: Paulina Chen
Federal Resume Samples: Susanne James (Derived Preference Military Spouse), Bobbi Rossiter (Military
    Spouse), Natalie Skelton (Military Spouse / LinkedIn), Mariano Torres (Veteran), Dan Kim (Networking Job
    Fair Resume), Toran Gaal (Wounded Warrior excerpts), Suzanne James (Introduction Sample), and April
    Piper and Brian Lawson (Step 6 Before and Afters)
Federal Staffing, Veteran Preference, and Schedule A SMEs: Charles Clark (USAF Retired), Ligaya Fernandez,
    and Josephine Barrientos
Intelligence and DOD Agency Lists: Ellen Lazarus
Updates on Agency List and Chapters: John Gagnon, Ph.D., J.D.
Program S Contributor: Bobbi Rossiter
Wounded Warrior Technical Consulting: Dennis Eley, Jr.
Curriculum Design: Emily Troutman, MPP
Photographs: Brian Lieberman, Bigwave Digital Services, Maui, Hawaii
Copyediting: Pamela Sikora
Index: Connie Binder

Table of Contents

This book actually works, and I am not just saying that because I worked on this book.

I have helped design and edit many of the previous editions of the *Jobseeker's Guide*, but this time was different. This time, I actually applied for and got my dream federal job using the very same Ten Steps that you hold in your hands right now.

The funny thing is that I started off my "federal job search" by doing research for this eighth edition. When OPM updated USAJOBS in August 2016, I jumped on the website to check out the changes for this book. I ended up following the rabbit all the way into the rabbit hole until I received a federal job offer!

Here are a few tidbits that I have learned along the way:

Step 1 - Research the Federal Job Search Process

The more you know, the better your chances of success. For example, I had worked as a GS-13 before, but I was willing to apply for a GS-12 based on the pay range, and I knew I had an even better chance of landing a GS-12 job. Also, I was hired into a different organization than I previously worked in, but the missions are related, and that helped my application as well.

Step 2 - Networking

I did not network to find this position, but networking played a key role in my job search nonetheless. I had to ask for help from many different people: for information, for references, and for smoothly processing my application and hiring. In fact, good networking skills are critical for overall career success.

Step 3 - Research Vacancy Announcements on USAJOBS

You will have to spend time playing around with your search criteria to get the right combination of flexibility and specificity. When I finally figured out what worked for me, my search results ended up usually being about eight screens long. It was tedious to sort through the listings every time I refreshed my search, so I figured out that I could sort the list according to the posting dates and just check the end of the list every day or two. With minimal effort, I found three announcements that matched my skills even though they have very different titles: Visual Information Specialist, Technical Editor, and Training Manager.

Want to know my favorite tip on reading vacancy announcements? Do a treasure hunt search for the link in the announcement that says "View the Questionnaire" (or similar phrase). Here is your magic list of the knowledge, skills, and abilities for the job announcement. If you cannot answer E or Expert for at least 85% of those questions, then you need not apply. Getting closer to 95% is even better. It is important to neither deflate nor inflate your answers, though most people tend to shortchange themselves by deflating their answers. Remember to support your answers in your resume.

Step 4 - Analyze Vacancy Announcements for Keywords

Keywords are actually a part of step 3 (announcement research), but they are so important that they deserve their very own step. You absolutely must hit the keywords from the job announcement in your resume. The problem is that every announcement has different keywords, which means that every resume you submit should be different. Yes, it is a lot of work, but you will experience 0% success unless you submit to this truth.

Step 5 – Analyze Your Core Competencies

Core competencies are sourced both from who you are as well as from the keywords in the job announcement. For example, I always include written communication as one of my core competencies in every resume, because it is one of my stronger skills, but when it is a keyword in a job announcement, I give it additional attention and air time in my resume.

Step 6 – Write Your Outline Format and Paper Federal Resumes

The Outline Format is the most effective format for your federal resume, not only because it is easy to read, but also because it is easy to adapt for different vacancy announcement keywords. If you want to read a fun and easy explanation of the Outline Format, check out my blog post *Help Me Hire a Minion*: www.resume-place.com/2013/10/help-me-hire-a-minion/.

Step 7 – KSAs, Accomplishments, and Questionnaires

Accomplishments are not optional. I find them to be most important when you are referred and the hiring manager reviews your resume. When viewed among the best of the best candidates, your accomplishment stories will make you memorable. They are also the launching point to a successful interview. I included in my resume that we won six book awards for books I designed last year, and this became a discussion point in my interviews.

Step 8 – Apply for Jobs in USAJOBS

I submitted my resume using the upload resume feature in USAJOBS. However, I am considered an advanced "submitter." If you are a beginner, I highly recommended that you use the resume builder for your first or second drive out until you learn the important rules of the road.

Step 9 – Track and Follow Up

Selected

I love the new colored application status graphics on the USAJOBS website, especially because I did not receive notification emails. In some cases, the USAJOBS website had extremely up-to-the-minute information.

Step 10 – Interviewing & The Best Secret in All of Federal Hiring

I went through all nine yards of the interview process: a phone interview (60 minutes), a writing sample submission, AND an in-person behavior-based interview (90 minutes). I survived this arduous journey with the help of the interview tips in this book and our other publications.

I was the very fortunate person to be the first to read and test the brand-new "negotiating your job offer" techniques we added to this edition, and I am happy to tell you that I achieved 100% success with the submission of a Superior Qualifications Letter. This negotiation information alone makes this book worth buying. We think that, currently, you will not find this information anywhere else in the world.

May the Ten Steps be with you on your own federal job hunt!

With thanks to Kathryn and the Resume Place for the opportunity help federal jobseekers worldwide,

Paulina Chen
Developmental Editing and Interior Page Layout

1. Review the federal job process. Your federal job search is a campaign, so set up your strategy for search right now. Learn which federal job is right for you based on the qualifications and education required. Find out what grade level and salary you qualify for.

2. Network —Who do you know? For Competitive and Non-Competitive federal positions, prepare a targeted resume and cover letter and begin your search ahead of the USAJOBS campaign.

3. Research vacancy announcements on USAJOBS. Before you write your federal resume, look for positions that match your qualifications and education. Read the Duties and Qualifications sections of the announcements and become familiar with the required work in government.

4. Analyze vacancy announcements for keywords. You can find keywords in the Duties and Specialized Experience sections of the announcements, as well as in the list of KSAs and the Questionnaire, which may appear in the right-hand toggle menus How to Apply or Required Documents. Learn how to add keywords to your resume.

5. Analyze your core competencies. Do you have great customer services skills? Excellent interpersonal and problem-solving skills? Are you a team player? Are you a good analyst? Add these "soft" skills to your resume to stand out with a hiring manager.

6. Write your Outline Format and paper federal resumes. Learn how to write your resume using small paragraphs, ALL CAP KEYWORDS, and accomplishments in the CCAR format. This is the perfect combination of duties and accomplishments to demonstrate your qualifications. The Outline Format resume is easy to change for additional job announcements.

7. KSAs, accomplishments, and questionnaires. The Self-Assessment Questionnaire—the second part of a USAJOBS application—is very important. THIS IS A TEST, and the resume must match! The Questionnaire asks about the required Knowledge, Skills, and Abilities (KSAs) for the job. Accomplishments in your resume can prove the KSAs that you have.

8. Apply for jobs on USAJOBS. Set up a USAJOBS account; complete the Profile section; upload your supporting documents; copy and paste your resume into the USAJOBS Builder; and then answer the Self-Assessment questions. The online application is complicated, and you need practice. As you apply for more positions, you will get better!

9. Track and follow up on your application. With this feature in USAJOBS, you can check to see what happened with your application. Find out if your application was RECEIVED, INCOMPLETE, or REFERRED (a great result!).

10. Interview for a federal job. THIS IS ANOTHER TEST. Make sure you are prepared to tell your best accomplishment stories in the Behavior-Based Structured Interview. This interview is an oral examination and you must prepare, practice, and be ready to impress one or more hiring managers.

What's New in the 8th Edition of the Jobseeker's Guide

Everyone wears different "hats" at work. You can also think about the your skills or leadership in different disciplines or programs. These hats and disciplines are KEYWORDS for your federal resume. Make a list of five to seven hats you wear every day in your job to form the basis of your Outline Format federal resume in Steps 5 and 6 of this guide.

Examples of hats:

- Supply Analyst
- Logistics Manager
- Transportation Specialist
- Supervisor
- Instructor
- Team Leader
- Database Administrator
- Research / Analyst
- Contract Officer
- Purchasing Specialist
- Office Administrator
- Advisor
- Computer Operations
- Customer Services

Your list of hats:

_____

_____

_____

_____

_____

_____

It's time to brag a little about how good you are at your work! Write about a situation, project or problem that you faced in your current or recent position. It is important to make your resume interesting for Human Resources reviewers and managers in order to get referred or selected for an interview!

Describe an accomplishment from your current position or recent volunteer work. Accomplishments are critical for your federal resume, assessment questionnaire essays / examples, and Behavior-Based Interviews.

Write at least three sentences here about your accomplishment:

Write your story with the
Resume Place accomplishment tool:
www.resume-place.com/ccar_accomplishment

This military spouse with Derived Preference needs an easy-to-read administrative resume with her top Knowledge, Skills, and Abilities featured with KEYWORDS. We also added accomplishments to stand out with the human resources reviewer and hiring manager.

Work Experience:
AFBA Armed Forces Benefit Association
909 N Washington Street
Alexandria, VA   22314 United States

09/2014 - Present
Salary: 60,000.00 USD Per Year
Hours per week: 40
New Business Analyst

Duties, Accomplishments and Related Skills:
PROCESS APPLICATIONS for insurance policies with a total value between $80-$200 million per month, following strict underwriting guidelines and ensuring federal and state regulations and laws are properly followed. Analyze applications and forward to medical underwriters when necessary. Update and verify customer information in LifePro and AS400 databases.

COMMUNICATE IN WRITTEN AND ORAL FORM to customers and staff to obtain additional information regarding over 1,000 new applications monthly. Provide status updates to staff and inform leadership of issues requiring attention. Review and acknowledge beneficiary change forms and other legal documents submitted by customers ensuring policies, regulations and laws are adhered to. Provide feedback to management regarding system problems and trends.

DELIVER OUTSTANDING CUSTOMER SERVICE by notifying 50-100 customers per month facing decrease in coverage via mail. Ensure correspondence is clear, concise and grammatically correct. Communicate with customers via phone and mail, providing customers with information on changes and options. Utilize tact and diplomacy to establish trust and rapport, resulting in upgrades of coverage in 50-80% of policies.

TRACK, MAINTAIN AND ANALYZE DATA on customer lapsed policies utilizing Microsoft Excel spreadsheet, analyzing for determination of reinstatement or termination resulting in reinstatement of up to 60% of accounts. Report required actions, based on analysis, to the accounting department for resolution. Retain long-time customers by manually maintaining a detailed spreadsheet of older policies and making adjustments of workflows in Salesforce Customer Relation Management System (CRS) and coordination through LifePro.

WRITE, EDIT AND PREPARE REPORTS AND CORRESPONDENCE relating to policies, beneficiaries, application status, and workflows. Prepare reports utilizing Salesforce, LifePro and AS400.

KEY ACCOMPLISHMENTS:

ANALYZED ADMINISTRATIVE PRACTICES AND PROPOSED IMPROVEMENTS to ensure maximum productivity in the New Business department.

- Giving staff an additional computer monitor (to process each case we use multiple screens for AS400, ID3, Salesforce, LifePro and Image besides Accurint and Lotus notes for e-mail). Time saved per case: 2-5 minutes. This means, if we process 50 cases and save 1-2 hours, we can easily process 10-20 more cases that day.

- Specific queues to target certain actions to avoid unnecessary volume increase and delay of cases that are ready to be approved. Those "special action" cases were sent to people's personal queues or pended by people who did not know what to do--and therefore were neglected. With the specific queue system, for example, if a different rate was offered (e.g., tob status or graded instead of preferred due to medical history), instead of being pended in the general queue it would go to the "Rate queue".
  Time saved: 5-10 cases per day in a queue can all be worked together instead of pended for days if not weeks.

DESIGNED NEW SPREADSHEET FOR MEDICAL REJECT RECORDS
Designed a new Spreadsheet for Medical Reject records for the Medical Underwriters to utilize in reviewing cases before they are sent to our external underwriter. This helps Medical Underwriters review problem cases daily instead of reviewing an entire medical queue of cases/ issues less often. It also prevents jet-issuing before thoroughly checking; therefore, it saves time and trouble later on because there is less need to obtain medical information from the hospital or doctor's office.

You can apply for federal jobs BEFORE you retire or separate!

How to Apply for Federal Positions within 120 days of Separation or Retirement

- The military separatee or retiree will need a Proof of Service or Statement of Service letter from their Executive Officer or military personnel office.

- Military separatees and retirees (except for military retirees applying for DOD positions: see 180-Day Waiver below) can apply for federal positions within 120 days of separation or retirement.

- A military retiree who is 120 days from retirement CAN apply to non-DOD agencies, such as the FBI, DOC, or DOT, using the Proof or Statement of Service.

- Make sure to upload your Proof or Statement of Service, with a copy of your separation or retirement order, into your USAJOBS documents.

- When you receive your DD-214, upload it, then delete your Proof or Statement of Service and separation or retirement order.

180-Day Waiver Needed for Retirees to Begin a DOD Job

- NEW! Based on the National Defense Authorization Act of FY2017 signed December 23, 2016, retiring military personnel cannot begin federal employment with a Department of Defense agency until 180 days past their retirement date.

- Exceptions to this policy will require the DOD agency to submit a waiver to the 180-day policy proving that there were no non-vet applicants qualified to fill the position under normal merit rules.

- Members should not assume that they can submit/request the 180-day waiver; submission is up to the agency.

- Read the guidance on the 180-day waiver policy here: http://www.resume-place.com/resources/.

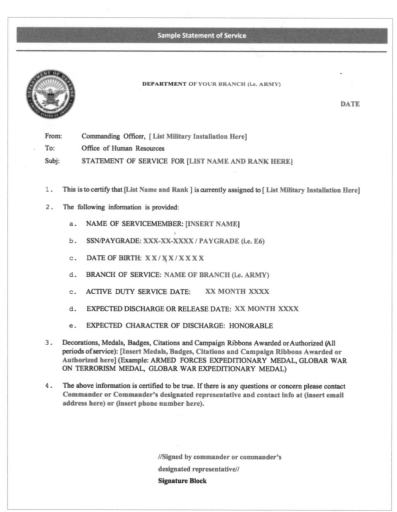

Sample Statement of Service

DEPARTMENT OF YOUR BRANCH (I.e. ARMY)

DATE

From: Commanding Officer, [List Military Installation Here]
To: Office of Human Resources
Subj: STATEMENT OF SERVICE FOR [LIST NAME AND RANK HERE]

1. This is to certify that [List Name and Rank] is currently assigned to [List Military Installation Here]

2. The following information is provided:

    a. NAME OF SERVICEMEMBER: [INSERT NAME]

    b. SSN/PAYGRADE: XXX-XX-XXXX / PAYGRADE (i.e. E6)

    c. DATE OF BIRTH: XX / XX / XXXX

    d. BRANCH OF SERVICE: NAME OF BRANCH (I.e. ARMY)

    c. ACTIVE DUTY SERVICE DATE: XX MONTH XXXX

    d. EXPECTED DISCHARGE OR RELEASE DATE: XX MONTH XXXX

    e. EXPECTED CHARACTER OF DISCHARGE: HONORABLE

3. Decorations, Medals, Badges, Citations and Campaign Ribbons Awarded or Authorized (All periods of service): [Insert Medals, Badges, Citations and Campaign Ribbons Awarded or Authorized here] (Example: ARMED FORCES EXPEDITIONARY MEDAL, GLOBAR WAR ON TERRORISM MEDAL, GLOBAR WAR EXPEDITIONARY MEDAL)

4. The above information is certified to be true. If there is any questions or concern please contact Commander or Commander's designated representative and contact info at (insert email address here) or (insert phone number here).

//Signed by commander or commander's designated representative//
Signature Block

Priority Placement Program – S

Military spouses can apply for federal positions with the Department of Defense's Priority Placement Program – S (PPP-S, E.O. 13473) with indefinite registration.

Good News! The National Defense Authorization Act of FY 2017 eliminated the two-year limitation for PPP registrations. Now, a military spouse with E.O. 13473 appointability can be registered in the PPP resume database until something happens to eliminate their eligibility, e.g. if they are hired into a federal position. NOTE: Military spouses whose eligibility terminated before 23 December 2016 are not eligible for reinstatement of their eligibility.

The Ten Steps to a Federal Job® federal resume writing methods also apply to the PPP-S resume application. More on PPP-S in *The Stars Are Lined Up for Military Spouses* by Kathryn Troutman, coming in 2017.

Noncompetitive Appointment of Certain Military Spouses

Executive Order 13473, dated September 28, 2008, authorized the noncompetitive appointment of certain military spouses to competitive service positions. http://www.gpo.gov/fdsys/pkg/FR-2008-09-30/pdf/E8-23125.pdf. See also https://www.congress.gov/bill/114th-congress/senate-bill/2943/text.

Executive Order 12568 - Military Spouse Preference (MSP)

The spouse of an active duty member of the Military Services (including the U.S. Coast Guard and full-time Reserve or National Guard), who relocates via a permanent change of station (PCS) move as a sponsored dependent to the military sponsor's new permanent duty station, is entitled to military spouse preference (MSP) for all positions in the commuting area of the new duty station being filled under competitive procedures.

REQUEST AND AUTHORIZATION FOR PERMANENT CHANGE OF STATION - MILITARY

PRIVACY ACT STATEMENT

AUTHORITY: 10 U.S.C. 8013, Secretary of the Air Force E.O. 9397 (SSN) as amended. Powers and duties; delegation by 8032,General duties; implemented by Air Force Instruction 36-2102, Base-level Relocation Procedures.
PURPOSE: Each type of relocation of Air Force personnel requires specific actions described either on a checklist or by sending a form letter to the applicable base activity having a responsibility for ensuring accomplishment of the action.
ROUTINE USES: In addition to those disclosures generally under 5 U.S.C. 552a(b) of the Privacy Act, these records or information contained therein may specifically be disclosed outside the DoD as a routine use pursuant to 5 U.S.C. 552a(b)3. 'Blanket Routine Uses' apply.
DISCLOSURE: VOLUNTARY: SSN is used to reference member's official records. Failure to provide SSN may make it difficult for member to receive pay and entitlements in coordination with Permanent Change of Station.

The following individual will proceed on permanent change of station:	☐ PCS without PCA	☒ PCS with PCA	TED AUG 16
1. GRADE, NAME *(Last, First, Middle Initial)*	2. SSAN		3. SAFSC/CAFSC

4. SECURITY CLEARANCE *(include date of last investigation)* SCI(DCID 1/14 ELIGIBLE) SINGLE SCOPE BACKGROUND INVESTIGATION 20 DEC 2011	5. REPORT TO COMDR, NEW ASSIGNMENT	6. TRAVEL DAYS AUTHORIZED IF TRAVELING BY PRIVATELY - OWNED CONVEYANCE:

7. TDY ENROUTE

8. UNIT, MAJOR COMMAND AND ADDRESS OF UNIT FROM WHICH RELIEVED:	9. UNIT, MAJOR COMMAND AND ADDRESS OF UNIT TO BE ASSIGNED:

10. TYPE OF TOUR ☐ ACCOMPANIED ☐ UNACCOMPANIED *(Check One)* ☐ UNACCOMPANIED, DEPENDENTS RESTRICTED	11. TOUR LENGTH *(Total No. of Months)* 12. EXTENDED LONG TOUR VOL

13. DEPENDENT TRAVEL: ☐ A. CONCURRENT TRAVEL IS AUTOMATIC ☐ B. CONCURRENT TRAVEL IS APPROVED ☐ C. DEPENDENT TRAVEL IS DELAYED FOR LESS THAN 20 WEEKS ☐ D. DEPENDENT TRAVEL IS DELAYED FOR MORE THAN 20 WEEKS ☐ E. TRAVEL IS AUTHORIZED TO A DESIGNATED PLACE	14. THIS IS A JOIN-SPOUSE ASSIGNMENT *(Include spouse's grade, name & SSN)* NO
	15. AUTHORITY FOR CCTVL:

16. HOMEBASING/FOLLOW-ON ASSIGNMENT *(Include AAN, GPAS and RNLTD)*

17. DEPENDENT(s):*(List names, DOB of children, relationship to member and current address)*

Military spouses: Be sure to upload your PCS Order and marriage certificate into USAJOBS.

STEP

1

Review the Federal Job Process

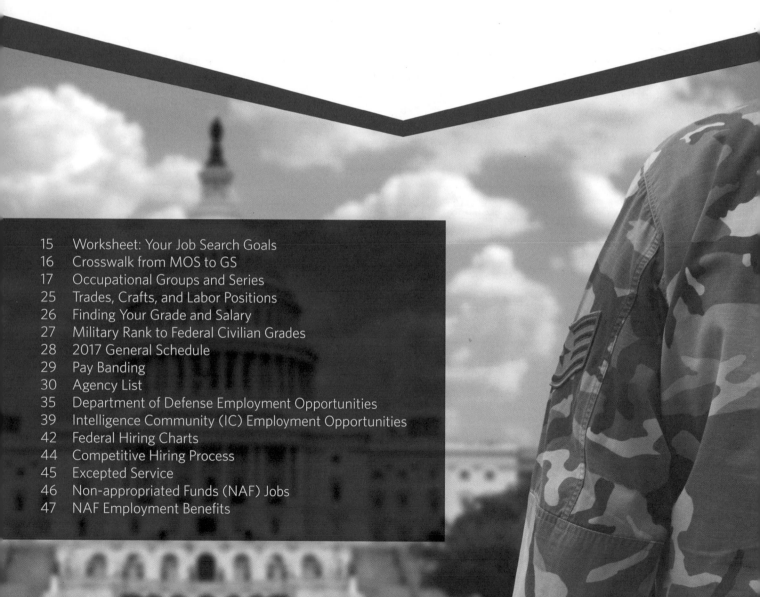

TARGET JOB TITLES AND SERIES

What is your current military job title?

How many years of specialized experience do you have?

Which federal job titles or series seem correct for you?

GRADE AND SALARY

What is your current military rank?

What is your current military salary?

What will be your target federal grade level?

What will your salary be, if you apply to a pay band agency?

TARGET AGENCIES

What are your target agencies?

TYPES OF FEDERAL JOBS

What types of federal jobs can you apply for and how will you apply for them?

This website is the first and only Military Occupational Code (MOC) to GS crosswalk and is sponsored by the State of Maryland. Match your MOC to GS interests online in just minutes!

Go to the Military to Federal Jobs Crosswalk: **www.mil2fedjobs.com**

Classification & Qualifications
CLASSIFYING GENERAL SCHEDULE POSITIONS

The list below contains the job titles from the HANDBOOK OF OCCUPATIONAL GROUPS AND FAMILIES, U.S. Office of Personnel Management Office of Classification, Washington, DC. See the full listing at: www.opm.gov/policy-data-oversight/classification-qualifications/classifying-general-schedule-positions/occupationalhandbook.pdf

Carefully reading the qualifications requirements for various occupational series at the different grades will help you make realistic decisions about what jobs to pursue (title, series, and grade) and may save you from wasting time applying for jobs where you simply don't meet those requirements.

GS-000 – MISCELLANEOUS OCCUPATIONS GROUP (NOT ELSEWHERE CLASSIFIED)

This group includes all classes of positions the duties of which are to administer, supervise, or perform work, which cannot be included in other occupational groups either because the duties are unique, or because they are complex and come in part under various groups.

Series in this group are:
GS-006 - Correctional Institution Administration Series
GS-007 - Correctional Officer Series
GS-011 - Bond Sales Promotion Series
GS-018 - Safety and Occupational Health Management Series
GS-019 - Safety Technician Series
GS-020 - Community Planning Series
GS-021 - Community Planning Technician Series
GS-023 - Outdoor Recreation Planning Series
GS-025 - Park Ranger Series
GS-028 - Environmental Protection Specialist Series
GS-029 - Environmental Protection Assistant Series
GS-030 - Sports Specialist Series
GS-050 - Funeral Directing Series
GS-060 - Chaplain Series
GS-062 - Clothing Design Series
GS-072 - Fingerprint Identification Series
GS-080 - Security Administration Series
GS-081 - Fire Protection and Prevention Series
GS-082 - United States Marshal Series
GS-083 - Police Series
GS-084 - Nuclear Materials Courier Series
GS-085 - Security Guard Series
GS-086 - Security Clerical and Assistance Series
GS-090 - Guide Series
GS-095 - Foreign Law Specialist Series
GS-099 - General Student Trainee Series

GS-100 – SOCIAL SCIENCE, PSYCHOLOGY, AND WELFARE GROUP

This group includes all classes of positions the duties of which are to advise on, administer, supervise, or perform research or other professional and scientific work, subordinate technical work, or related clerical work in one or more of the social sciences; in psychology; in social work; in recreational activities; or in the administration of public welfare and insurance programs.

Series in this group are:
GS-101 - Social Science Series
GS-102 - Social Science Aid and Technician Series
GS-105 - Social Insurance Administration Series
GS-106 - Unemployment Insurance Series
GS-107 - Health Insurance Administration Series
GS-110 - Economist Series
GS-119 - Economics Assistant Series
GS-130 - Foreign Affairs Series
GS-131 - International Relations Series
GS-132 - Intelligence Series
GS-134 - Intelligence Aid and Clerk Series
GS-135 - Foreign Agricultural Affairs Series
GS-136 - International Cooperation Series
GS-140 - Manpower Research and Analysis Series
GS-142 - Manpower Development Series
GS-150 - Geography Series
GS-160 - Civil Rights Analysis Series
GS-170 - History Series
GS-180 - Psychology Series
GS-181 - Psychology Aid and Technician Series
GS-184 - Sociology Series
GS-185 - Social Work Series
GS-186 - Social Services Aid and Assistant Series
GS-187 - Social Services Series
GS-188 - Recreation Specialist Series
GS-189 - Recreation Aid and Assistant Series
GS-190 - General Anthropology Series
GS-193 - Archeology Series
GS-199 - Social Science Student Trainee Series

GS-200 – HUMAN RESOURCES MANAGEMENT GROUP

This group includes all classes of positions the duties of which are to advise on, administer, supervise, or perform work involved in the various phases of human resources management.

Series in this group are:
GS-201 - Human Resources Management Series
GS-203 - Human Resources Assistance Series
GS-241 - Mediation Series
GS-243 - Apprenticeship and Training Series
GS-244 - Labor Management Relations Examining Series
GS-260 - Equal Employment Opportunity Series
GS-299 - Human Resources Management Student Trainee Series

GS-300 – GENERAL ADMINISTRATIVE, CLERICAL, AND OFFICE SERVICES GROUP

This group includes all classes of positions the duties of which are to administer, supervise, or perform work involved in management analysis; stenography, typing, correspondence, and secretarial work; mail and file work; the operation of office appliances; the operation of communications equipment, use of codes and ciphers, and procurement of the most effective and efficient communications services; the operation of microform equipment, peripheral equipment, mail processing equipment, duplicating equipment, and copier/duplicating equipment; and other work of a general clerical and administrative nature.

Series in this group are:
GS-301 - Miscellaneous Administration and Program Series
GS-302 - Messenger Series
GS-303 - Miscellaneous Clerk and Assistant Series
GS-304 - Information Receptionist Series
GS-305 - Mail and File Series
GS-309 - Correspondence Clerk Series
GS-312 - Clerk-Stenographer and Reporter Series
GS-313 - Work Unit Supervising Series
GS-318 - Secretary Series
GS-319 - Closed Microphone Reporting Series
GS-322 - Clerk-Typist Series
GS-326 - Office Automation Clerical and Assistance Series

GS-332 - Computer Operation Series
GS-335 - Computer Clerk and Assistant Series
GS-340 - Program Management Series
GS-341 - Administrative Officer Series
GS-342 - Support Services Administration Series
GS-343 - Management and Program Analysis Series
GS-344 - Management and Program Clerical and Assistance Series
GS-346 - Logistics Management Series
GS-350 - Equipment Operator Series
GS-356 - Data Transcriber Series
GS-357 - Coding Series
GS-360 - Equal Opportunity Compliance Series
GS-361 - Equal Opportunity Assistance Series
GS-382 - Telephone Operating Series
GS-390 - Telecommunications Processing Series
GS-391 - Telecommunications Series
GS-392 - General Telecommunications Series
GS-394 - Communications Clerical Series
GS-399 - Administration and Office Support Student Trainee Series

GS-400 – NATURAL RESOURCES MANAGEMENT AND BIOLOGICAL SCIENCES GROUP

This group includes all classes of positions the duties of which are to advise on, administer, supervise, or perform research or other professional and scientific work or subordinate technical work in any of the fields of science concerned with living organisms, their distribution, characteristics, life processes, and adaptations and relations to the environment; the soil, its properties and distribution, and the living organisms growing in or on the soil, and the management, conservation, or utilization thereof for particular purposes or uses.

Series in this group are:
GS-401 - General Natural Resources Management and Biological Sciences Series
GS-403 - Microbiology Series
GS-404 - Biological Science Technician Series
GS-405 - Pharmacology Series
GS-408 - Ecology Series
GS-410 - Zoology Series
GS-413 - Physiology Series
GS-414 - Entomology Series
GS-415 - Toxicology Series
GS-421 - Plant Protection Technician Series
GS-430 - Botany Series
GS-434 - Plant Pathology Series

GS-435 - Plant Physiology Series
GS-437 - Horticulture Series
GS-440 - Genetics Series
GS-454 - Rangeland Management Series
GS-455 - Range Technician Series
GS-457 - Soil Conservation Series
GS-458 - Soil Conservation Technician Series
GS-459 - Irrigation System Operation Series
GS-460 - Forestry Series
GS-462 - Forestry Technician Series
GS-470 - Soil Science Series
GS-471 - Agronomy Series
GS-480 - Fish and Wildlife Administration Series
GS-482 - Fish Biology Series
GS-485 - Wildlife Refuge Management Series
GS-486 - Wildlife Biology Series
GS-487 - Animal Science Series
GS-499 - Biological Science Student Trainee Series

GS-500 – ACCOUNTING AND BUDGET GROUP

This group includes all classes of positions the duties of which are to advise on, administer, supervise, or perform professional, technical, or related clerical work of an accounting, budget administration, related financial management or similar nature.

Series in this group are:
GS-501 - Financial Administration and Program
            Series
GS-503 - Financial Clerical and Technician Series
GS-505 - Financial Management Series
GS-510 - Accounting Series
GS-511 - Auditing Series
GS-512 - Internal Revenue Agent Series
GS-525 - Accounting Technician Series
GS-526 - Tax Specialist Series
GS-530 - Cash Processing Series
GS-540 - Voucher Examining Series
GS-544 - Civilian Pay Series
GS-545 - Military Pay Series
GS-560 - Budget Analysis Series
GS-561 - Budget Clerical and Assistance Series
GS-592 - Tax Examining Series
GS-593 - Insurance Accounts Series
GS-599 - Financial Management Student Trainee
            Series

GS-600 – MEDICAL, HOSPITAL, DENTAL, AND PUBLIC HEALTH GROUP

This group includes all classes of positions the duties of which are to advise on, administer, supervise or perform research or other professional and scientific work, subordinate technical work, or related clerical work in the several branches of medicine, surgery, and dentistry or in related patient care services such as dietetics, nursing, occupational therapy, physical therapy, pharmacy, and others.

Series in this group are:
GS-601 - General Health Science Series
GS-602 - Medical Officer Series
GS-603 - Physician's Assistant Series
GS-610 - Nurse Series
GS-620 - Practical Nurse Series
GS-621 - Nursing Assistant Series
GS-622 - Medical Supply Aide and Technician Series
GS-625 - Autopsy Assistant Series
GS-630 - Dietitian and Nutritionist Series
GS-631 - Occupational Therapist Series
GS-633 - Physical Therapist Series
GS-635 - Kinesiotherapy Series
GS-636 - Rehabilitation Therapy Assistant Series
GS-637 - Manual Arts Therapist Series
GS-638 - Recreation/Creative Arts Therapist Series
GS-639 - Educational Therapist Series
GS-640 - Health Aid and Technician Series
GS-642 - Nuclear Medicine Technician Series
GS-644 - Medical Technologist Series
GS-645 - Medical Technician Series
GS-646 - Pathology Technician Series
GS-647 - Diagnostic Radiologic Technologist Series
GS-648 - Therapeutic Radiologic Technologist
            Series
GS-649 - Medical Instrument Technician Series
GS-650 - Medical Technical Assistant Series
GS-651 - Respiratory Therapist Series
GS-660 - Pharmacist Series
GS-661 - Pharmacy Technician Series
GS-662 - Optometrist Series
GS-664 - Restoration Technician Series
GS-665 - Speech Pathology and Audiology Series
GS-667 - Orthotist and Prosthetist Series
GS-668 - Podiatrist Series
GS-669 - Medical Records Administration Series
GS-670 - Health System Administration Series
GS-671 - Health System Specialist Series
GS-672 - Prosthetic Representative Series

GS-673 - Hospital Housekeeping Management Series
GS-675 - Medical Records Technician Series
GS-679 - Medical Support Assistance Series
GS-680 - Dental Officer Series
GS-681 - Dental Assistant Series
GS-682 - Dental Hygiene Series
GS-683 - Dental Laboratory Aid and Technician Series
GS-685 - Public Health Program Specialist Series
GS-688 - Sanitarian Series
GS-690 - Industrial Hygiene Series
GS-696 - Consumer Safety Series
GS-698 - Environmental Health Technician Series
GS-699 - Medical and Health Student Trainee Series

GS-700 – VETERINARY MEDICAL SCIENCE GROUP

This group includes positions that advise on, administer, supervise, or perform professional or technical support work in the various branches of veterinary medical science.

Series in this group are:
GS-701 - Veterinary Medical Science Series
GS-704 - Animal Health Technician Series
GS-799 - Veterinary Student Trainee Series

GS-800 – ENGINEERING AND ARCHITECTURE GROUP

This group includes all classes of positions the duties of which are to advise on, administer, supervise, or perform professional, scientific, or technical work concerned with engineering or architectural projects, facilities, structures, systems, processes, equipment, devices, materials or methods. Positions in this group require knowledge of the science or art, or both, by which materials, natural resources, and power are made useful.

Series in this group are:
GS-801 - General Engineering Series
GS-802 - Engineering Technician Series
GS-803 - Safety Engineering Series
GS-804 - Fire Protection Engineering Series
GS-806 - Materials Engineering Series
GS-807 - Landscape Architecture Series
GS-808 - Architecture Series

GS-809 - Construction Control Technical Series
GS-810 - Civil Engineering Series
GS-817 - Survey Technical Series
GS-819 - Environmental Engineering Series
GS-828 - Construction Analyst Series
GS-830 - Mechanical Engineering Series
GS-840 - Nuclear Engineering Series
GS-850 - Electrical Engineering Series
GS-854 - Computer Engineering Series
GS-855 - Electronics Engineering Series
GS-856 - Electronics Technical Series
GS-858 - Biomedical Engineering Series
GS-861 - Aerospace Engineering Series
GS-871 - Naval Architecture Series
GS-873 - Marine Survey Technical Series
GS-880 - Mining Engineering Series
GS-881 - Petroleum Engineering Series
GS-890 - Agricultural Engineering Series
GS-892 - Ceramic Engineering Series
GS-893 - Chemical Engineering Series
GS-894 - Welding Engineering Series
GS-895 - Industrial Engineering Technical Series
GS-896 - Industrial Engineering Series
GS-899 - Engineering and Architecture Student Trainee Series

GS-900 – LEGAL AND KINDRED GROUP

This group includes all positions that advise on, administer, supervise, or perform work of a legal or kindred nature.

Series in this group are:
GS-901 - General Legal and Kindred Administration Series
GS-904 - Law Clerk Series
GS-905 - General Attorney Series
GS-920 - Estate Tax Examining Series
GS-930 - Hearings and Appeals Series
GS-945 - Clerk of Court Series
GS-950 - Paralegal Specialist Series
GS-958 - Employee Benefits Law Series
GS-962 - Contact Representative Series
GS-963 - Legal Instruments Examining Series
GS-965 - Land Law Examining Series
GS-967 - Passport and Visa Examining Series
GS-986 - Legal Assistance Series
GS-987 - Tax Law Specialist Series
GS-991 - Workers' Compensation Claims Examining Series
GS-993 - Railroad Retirement Claims Examining Series

GS-996 - Veterans Claims Examining Series
GS-998 - Claims Assistance and Examining Series
GS-999 - Legal Occupations Student Trainee Series

GS-1000 – INFORMATION AND ARTS GROUP

This group includes positions which involve professional, artistic, technical, or clerical work in (1) the communication of information and ideas through verbal, visual, or pictorial means, (2) the collection, custody, presentation, display, and interpretation of art works, cultural objects, and other artifacts, or (3) a branch of fine or applied arts such as industrial design, interior design, or musical composition. Positions in this group require writing, editing, and language ability; artistic skill and ability; knowledge of foreign languages; the ability to evaluate and interpret informational and cultural materials; or the practical application of technical or esthetic principles combined with manual skill and dexterity; or related clerical skills.

Series in this group are:
GS-1001 - General Arts and Information Series
GS-1008 - Interior Design Series
GS-1010 - Exhibits Specialist Series
GS-1015 - Museum Curator Series
GS-1016 - Museum Specialist and Technician Series
GS-1020 - Illustrating Series
GS-1021 - Office Drafting Series
GS-1035 - Public Affairs Series
GS-1040 - Language Specialist Series
GS-1046 - Language Clerical Series
GS-1051 - Music Specialist Series
GS-1054 - Theater Specialist Series
GS-1056 - Art Specialist Series
GS-1060 - Photography Series
GS-1071 - Audiovisual Production Series
GS-1082 - Writing and Editing Series
GS-1083 - Technical Writing and Editing Series
GS-1084 - Visual Information Series
GS-1087 - Editorial Assistance Series
GS-1099 - Information and Arts Student Trainee Series

GS-1100 – BUSINESS AND INDUSTRY GROUP

This group includes all classes of positions the duties of which are to advise on, administer, supervise, or perform work pertaining to and requiring a knowledge of business and trade practices, characteristics and use of equipment, products, or property, or industrial production methods and processes, including the conduct of investigations and studies; the collection, analysis, and dissemination of information; the establishment and maintenance of contacts with industry and commerce; the provision of advisory services; the examination and appraisement of merchandise or property; and the administration of regulatory provisions and controls.

Series in this group are:
GS-1101 - General Business and Industry Series
GS-1102 - Contracting Series
GS-1103 - Industrial Property Management Series
GS-1104 - Property Disposal Series
GS-1105 - Purchasing Series
GS-1106 - Procurement Clerical and Technician Series
GS-1107 - Property Disposal Clerical and Technician Series
GS-1130 - Public Utilities Specialist Series
GS-1140 - Trade Specialist Series
GS-1144 - Commissary Management Series
GS-1145 - Agricultural Program Specialist Series
GS-1146 - Agricultural Marketing Series
GS-1147 - Agricultural Market Reporting Series
GS-1150 - Industrial Specialist Series
GS-1152 - Production Control Series
GS-1160 - Financial Analysis Series
GS-1163 - Insurance Examining Series
GS-1165 - Loan Specialist Series
GS-1169 - Internal Revenue Officer Series
GS-1170 - Realty Series
GS-1171 - Appraising Series
GS-1173 - Housing Management Series
GS-1176 - Building Management Series
GS-1199 - Business and Industry Student Trainee Series

GS-1200 – COPYRIGHT, PATENT, AND TRADEMARK GROUP

This group includes all classes of positions the duties of which are to advise on, administer, supervise, or perform professional scientific, technical, and legal work involved in the cataloging and registration of copyrights, in the classification and issuance of patents, in the registration of trademarks, in the prosecution of applications for patents before the Patent Office, and in the giving of advice to Government officials on patent matters.

Series in this group are:
GS-1202 - Patent Technician Series
GS-1210 - Copyright Series
GS-1220 - Patent Administration Series
GS-1221 - Patent Adviser Series
GS-1222 - Patent Attorney Series
GS-1223 - Patent Classifying Series
GS-1224 - Patent Examining Series
GS-1226 - Design Patent Examining Series
GS-1299 - Copyright and Patent Student Trainee
       Series

GS-1300 – PHYSICAL SCIENCES GROUP

This group includes all classes of positions the duties of which are to advise on, administer, supervise, or perform research or other professional and scientific work or subordinate technical work in any of the fields of science concerned with matter, energy, physical space, time, nature of physical measurement, and fundamental structural particles; and the nature of the physical environment.

Series in this group are:
GS-1301 - General Physical Science Series
GS-1306 - Health Physics Series
GS-1310 - Physics Series
GS-1311 - Physical Science Technician Series
GS-1313 - Geophysics Series
GS-1315 - Hydrology Series
GS-1316 - Hydrologic Technician Series
GS-1320 - Chemistry Series
GS-1321 - Metallurgy Series
GS-1330 - Astronomy and Space Science Series
GS-1340 - Meteorology Series
GS-1341 - Meteorological Technician Series
GS-1350 - Geology Series

GS-1360 - Oceanography Series
GS-1361 - Navigational Information Series
GS-1370 - Cartography Series
GS-1371 - Cartographic Technician Series
GS-1372 - Geodesy Series
GS-1373 - Land Surveying Series
GS-1374 - Geodetic Technician Series
GS-1380 - Forest Products Technology Series
GS-1382 - Food Technology Series
GS-1384 - Textile Technology Series
GS-1386 - Photographic Technology Series
GS-1397 - Document Analysis Series
GS-1399 - Physical Science Student Trainee Series

GS-1400 – LIBRARY AND ARCHIVES GROUP

This group includes all classes of positions the duties of which are to advise on, administer, supervise, or perform professional and scientific work or subordinate technical work in the various phases of library and archival science.

Series in this group are:
GS-1410 - Librarian Series
GS-1411 - Library Technician Series
GS-1412 - Technical Information Services Series
GS-1420 - Archivist Series
GS-1421 - Archives Technician Series
GS-1499 - Library and Archives Student Trainee
       Series

GS-1500 – MATHEMATICS AND STATISTICS GROUP

This group includes all classes of positions the duties of which are to advise on, administer, supervise, or perform professional and scientific work or related clerical work in basic mathematical principles, methods, procedures, or relationships, including the development and application of mathematical methods for the investigation and solution of problems; the development and application of statistical theory in the selection, collection, classification, adjustment, analysis, and interpretation of data; the development and application of mathematical, statistical, and financial principles to programs or problems involving life and property risks; and any other professional and scientific or related clerical work requiring primarily and mainly the understanding and use of mathematical theories, methods, and operations.

Series in this group are:
GS-1501 - General Mathematics and Statistics Series
GS-1510 - Actuarial Science Series
GS-1515 - Operations Research Series
GS-1520 - Mathematics Series
GS-1521 - Mathematics Technician Series
GS-1529 - Mathematical Statistics Series
GS-1530 - Statistics Series
GS-1531 - Statistical Assistant Series
GS-1540 - Cryptography Series
GS-1541 - Cryptanalysis Series
GS-1550 - Computer Science Series
GS-1599 - Mathematics and Statistics Student Trainee Series

GS-1600 – EQUIPMENT, FACILITIES, AND SERVICES GROUP

This group includes positions the duties of which are to advise on, manage, or provide instructions and information concerning the operation, maintenance, and use of equipment, shops, buildings, laundries, printing plants, power plants, cemeteries, or other government facilities, or other work involving services provided predominantly by persons in trades. Positions in this group require technical or managerial knowledge and ability, plus a practical knowledge of trades, crafts, or manual labor operations.

Series in this group are:
GS-1601 - Equipment, Facilities, and Services Series
GS-1603 - Equipment, Facilities, and Services Assistance Series
GS-1630 - Cemetery Administration Services Series
GS-1640 - Facility Operations Services Series
GS-1654 - Printing Services Series
GS-1658 - Laundry Operations Services Series
GS-1667 - Food Services Series
GS-1670 - Equipment Services Series
GS-1699 - Equipment, Facilities, and Services Student Trainee Series

GS-1700 – EDUCATION GROUP

This group includes positions that involve administering, managing, supervising, performing, or supporting education or training work when the paramount requirement of the position is knowledge of, or skill in, education, training, or instruction processes.

Series in this group are:
GS-1701 - General Education and Training Series
GS-1702 - Education and Training Technician Series
GS-1710 - Education and Vocational Training Series
GS-1712 - Training Instruction Series
GS-1715 - Vocational Rehabilitation Series
GS-1720 - Education Program Series
GS-1725 - Public Health Educator Series
GS-1730 - Education Research Series
GS-1740 - Education Services Series
GS-1750 - Instructional Systems Series
GS-1799 - Education Student Trainee Series

GS-1800 – INVESTIGATION GROUP

This group includes all classes of positions the duties of which are to advise on, administer, supervise, or perform investigation, inspection, or enforcement work primarily concerned with alleged or suspected offenses against the laws of the United States, or such work primarily concerned with determining compliance with laws and regulations.

Series in this group are:
GS-1801 - General Inspection, Investigation, and Compliance Series
GS-1802 - Compliance Inspection and Support Series
GS-1810 - General Investigating Series
GS-1811 - Criminal Investigating Series
GS-1812 - Game Law Enforcement Series
GS-1815 - Air Safety Investigating Series
GS-1816 - Immigration Inspection Series
GS-1822 - Mine Safety and Health Series
GS-1825 - Aviation Safety Series
GS-1831 - Securities Compliance Examining Series
GS-1850 - Agricultural Commodity Warehouse Examining Series
GS-1854 - Alcohol, Tobacco and Firearms Inspection Series
GS-1862 - Consumer Safety Inspection Series
GS-1863 - Food Inspection Series
GS-1864 - Public Health Quarantine Inspection Series
GS-1881 - Customs and Border Protection Interdiction Series
GS-1884 - Customs Patrol Officer Series
GS-1889 - Import Specialist Series
GS-1890 - Customs Inspection Series
GS-1894 - Customs Entry and Liquidating Series

GS-1895 - Customs and Border Protection Series
GS-1896 - Border Patrol Agent Series
GS-1897 - Customs Aid Series
GS-1899 - Investigation Student Trainee Series

GS-1900 – QUALITY ASSURANCE, INSPECTION, AND GRADING GROUP

This group includes all classes of positions the duties of which are advise on, supervise, or perform administrative or technical work primarily concerned with the quality assurance or inspection of material, facilities, and processes; or with the grading of commodities under official standards.

Series in this group are:
GS-1910 - Quality Assurance Series
GS-1980 - Agricultural Commodity Grading Series
GS-1981 - Agricultural Commodity Aid Series
GS-1999 - Quality Inspection Student Trainee Series

GS-2000 – SUPPLY GROUP

This group includes positions that involve work concerned with furnishing all types of supplies, equipment, material, property (except real estate), and certain services to components of the federal government, industrial, or other concerns under contract to the government, or receiving supplies from the federal government. Included are positions concerned with one or more aspects of supply activities from initial planning, including requirements analysis and determination, through acquisition, cataloging, storage, distribution, utilization to ultimate issues for consumption or disposal. The work requires a knowledge of one or more elements or parts of a supply system, and/or supply methods, policies, or procedures.

Series in this group are:
GS-2001 - General Supply Series
GS-2003 - Supply Program Management Series
GS-2005 - Supply Clerical and Technician Series
GS-2010 - Inventory Management Series
GS-2030 - Distribution Facilities and Storage Management Series
GS-2032 - Packaging Series

GS-2050 - Supply Cataloging Series
GS-2091 - Sales Store Clerical Series
GS-2099 - Supply Student Trainee Series

GS-2100 – TRANSPORTATION GROUP

This group includes all classes of positions the duties of which are to advise on, administer, supervise, or perform clerical, administrative, or technical work involved in the provision of transportation service to the government, the regulation of transportation utilities by the government, or the management of government-funded transportation programs, including transportation research and development projects.

Series in this group are:
GS-2101 - Transportation Specialist Series
GS-2102 - Transportation Clerk and Assistant Series
GS-2110 - Transportation Industry Analysis Series
GS-2121 - Railroad Safety Series
GS-2123 - Motor Carrier Safety Series
GS-2125 - Highway Safety Series
GS-2130 - Traffic Management Series
GS-2131 - Freight Rate Series
GS-2135 - Transportation Loss and Damage Claims Examining Series
GS-2144 - Cargo Scheduling Series
GS-2150 - Transportation Operations Series
GS-2151 - Dispatching Series
GS-2152 - Air Traffic Control Series
GS-2154 - Air Traffic Assistance Series
GS-2161 - Marine Cargo Series
GS-2181 - Aircraft Operation Series
GS-2183 - Air Navigation Series
GS-2185 - Aircrew Technician Series
GS-2199 - Transportation Student Trainee Series

GS-2200 – INFORMATION TECHNOLOGY GROUP

Series in this group are:
GS-2210 - Information Technology Management Series
GS-2299 - Information Technology Student Trainee series

Federal Classification and Job Grading Systems

| ▶ Main | Job Grading Standards for |
| ▶ White Collar Positions | Trades, Craft, and Labor Positions |

www.opm.gov/fedclass/html/fwseries.asp

2500 Wire Communications Equipment Installation and Maintenance Group
2600 Electronic Equipment Installation and Maintenance Group
2800 Electrical Installation and Maintenance Group
3100 Fabric and Leather Work Group
3300 Instrument Work Group
3400 Machine Tool Work Group
3500 General Services and Support Work Group
3600 Structural and Finishing Work Group
3700 Metal Processing Group
3800 Metal Work Group
3900 Motion Picture, Radio, Television, and Sound Equipment Operating Group
4100 Painting and Paperhanging Group
4200 Plumbing and Pipefitting Group
4300 Pliable Materials Work Group
4400 Printing Group
4600 Wood Work Group
4700 General Maintenance and Operations Work Group
4800 General Equipment Maintenance Group
5000 Plant and Animal Work Group
5200 Miscellaneous Occupations Group
5300 Industrial Equipment Maintenance Group
5400 Industrial Equipment Operation Group
5700 Transportation/Mobile Equipment Operation Group
5800 Transportation/Mobile Equipment Maintenance Group
6500 Ammunition, Explosives, and Toxic Materials Work Group
6600 Armament Work Group
6900 Warehousing and Stock Handling Group
7000 Packing and Processing Group
7300 Laundry, Dry Cleaning, and Pressing Group
7400 Food Preparation and Serving Group
7600 Personal Services Group
8200 Fluid Systems Maintenance Group
8600 Engine Overhaul Group
8800 Aircraft Overhaul Group

The human resources staffing specialist will determine your qualifications for the position by looking at the following items in your federal resume. Qualification determinations are based on:

EXPERIENCE
- ➤ Quality of experience
  - • Directly related to the job or general nature of work
  - • Complexity of assignments (what, for whom, why)
  - • Decision-making authority or span of control
  - • Knowledge, skills, and abilities used
- ➤ Length of experience
  - • Full-time or part-time
  - • Number of hours per week

EDUCATION
- ➤ Major field of study
- ➤ Number of years completed or number of semester hours completed
- ➤ GPA

TRAINING
- ➤ Related to job
- ➤ Number of days or hours

Qualifying Based on Education Alone

GS-2:   High school graduation or equivalent (i.e., GED)

GS-3:   One year above high school

GS-4:   Two years above high school (or Associate's degree)

GS-5:   Bachelor's degree

GS 7:   One full year of graduate study or Bachelor's degree with superior academic achievement (GPA 2.95 or higher out of a possible 4.0)

GS-9:   Master's degree or equivalent such as J.D. or LL.B.

GS-11: Ph.D.

NOTE: There are exceptions to this chart; there are occupations that will not accept education in lieu of experience.

Determining the government grade level based on your military rank is challenging. Here are some ways to determine the appropriate grade:

- **Salary:** Match the salary you are earning now against the OPM General Schedule charts.
- **Specialized Experience:** Read USAJOBS announcements for the Specialized Experience required and see if you qualify for the grade level they are advertising.
- **Certification and Training**: Read job announcements and see if you have the specific certification and training required.

NOTE: This chart is not an official federal government grade to military rank conversion chart but an approximation based on our experience in analyzing rank against the requirements of USAJOBS vacancy announcements. Conversions may vary based on an agency's organizational structure, location, and/or size.

Federal Civilian Grade	Wage Grade	Military Commissioned Officer	Military Warrant Officer	Military Enlisted
Assistants				Trainee/Assistants
GS-2, 3, 4, 5	WG-2, 3, 4, 5			E-2, 3, 4
GS-6, 7, 8	WG-6, 7, 8			E-5, 6
Specialist/ Technician		Junior Leaders / First-Line Supervisors		Specialist/ First-Line Supervisors
GS-7	WG-9			E-3, 4
GS-9	WG-10	O-1		E-5, E-7
GS-11	WG-10	2	WO-1	E-5, E-7
GS-12	WG-10, 11, 12	3	WO-1	E-7
Team Lead/ Section Leader		Mid-Level Leader/ Section Manager		Operations Supervisor/ Supervisor of First-Line Supervisors
GS-12	WG-12	O-3, 4	WO-2	E-7, 8
GS-13	WG-12	4	3	E-8
Supervisor/ Branch Chief		Leader of Mid-Level Leaders /Manage Organizations		Superintendent/ Supervisor of Ops Supervisors
GS-13	WG-12, 13, 14	O-4	WO-4	E-8, 9
GS-14	WG-12, 13, 14	5	5	E-9
Manager		Senior Leader / Head of Organization		Senior Enl Advisor/ Career Field Manager
GS-14	WG-12, 13, 14	O-5	WO-5	
GS-15	WG-12, 13, 14	6		

Effective January 2017 – Annual Rates by Grade and Step

https://www.opm.gov/policy-data-oversight/pay-leave/salaries-wages/2017/general-schedule/

The General Schedule (GS) is a worldwide pay system that covers more than 1.5 million employees. The GS pay schedule has 15 grades and 10 steps in each grade covering more than 400 occupations.

Pay varies by geographic location: Be sure to look up your potential salary WITH your locality pay!

- Washington, DC / Baltimore: Add 27.10% to base salary
- San Diego, CA: Add 26.98% to base salary
- Hawaii: Add 17.92% to base salary and 11.32% for COLA

Grade	Step 1	Step 2	Step 3	Step 4	Step 5	Step 6	Step 7	Step 8	Step 9	Step 10	Within Grade
1	18526	19146	19762	20375	20991	21351	21960	22575	22599	23171	VARIES
2	20829	21325	22015	22599	22853	23525	24197	24869	25541	26213	VARIES
3	22727	23485	24243	25001	25759	26517	27275	28033	28791	29549	758
4	25514	26364	27214	28064	28914	29764	30614	31464	32314	33164	850
5	28545	29497	30449	31401	32353	33305	34257	35209	36161	37113	952
6	31819	32880	33941	35002	36063	37124	38185	39246	40307	41368	1061
7	35359	36538	37717	38896	40075	41254	42433	43612	44791	45970	1179
8	39159	40464	41769	43074	44379	45684	46989	48294	49599	50904	1305
9	43251	44693	46135	47577	49019	50461	51903	53345	54787	56229	1442
10	47630	49218	50806	52394	53982	55570	57158	58746	60334	61922	1588
11	52329	54073	55817	57561	59305	61049	62793	64537	66281	68025	1744
12	62722	64813	66904	68995	71086	73177	75268	77359	79450	81541	2091
13	74584	77070	79556	82042	84528	87014	89500	91986	94472	96958	2486
14	88136	91074	94012	96950	99888	102826	105764	108702	111640	114578	2938
15	103672	107128	110584	114040	117496	120952	124408	127864	131320	134776	3456

Not every agency follows the GS pay system anymore. "Pay banding," which allows an organization to combine two or more grades into a wider "band," is an increasingly popular alternative to the traditional GS system. The "grade" information for jobs in agencies using pay banding will have a different look, and that look may be specific to a particular agency. Don't be surprised to see something as odd as ZP-1 or NO-2 in place of GS-5 or GS-7. Focus on the duties, the salary, whether you are qualified for the job, and whether you would like to have it. Remember, the federal government is large, and needs a way to increase flexibility of pay based on performance. Pay bands are its answer.

Example of Pay Band Salaries:
Transportation Security Administration

https://hraccess.tsa.dhs.gov/hraccess/pdf/2016%20Core%20Compensation%20Bands%20 FINAL%2012-21-2015.pdf

Pay Band	Min	Max
A	17,601	25,734
B	20,164	29,410
C	22,839	34,312
D	26,291	39,437
E	30,190	45,340
F	34,646	52,024
G	40,552	62,830
H	49,462	76,644
I	60,268	93,465
J	73,527	113,963
K	87,896	136,244
L	105,052	160,300
M	123,879	160,300

Agency List

A

AbilityOne Commission
Access Board
Administration for Children and Families
Administration on Aging (AOA)
Administration for Community Living
Administration for Native Americans
Administration on Developmental Disabilities
Administrative Conference of the United States
Administrative Office of the U.S. Courts
Advisory Council on Historic Preservation
African Development Foundation
Agency for Healthcare Research and Quality
Agency for International Development
Agency for Toxic Substances and Disease Registry
Agricultural Marketing Service
Agricultural Research Service
Agriculture Department
Air Force
Air Force Reserve
Alcohol and Tobacco Tax and Trade Bureau
American Battle Monuments Commission
AmeriCorps
AMTRAK (National Railroad Passenger Corporation)
Animal and Plant Health Inspection Service
Appalachian Regional Commission
Architect of the Capitol
Arctic Research Commission
Armed Forces Retirement Home
Arms Control and International Security, Under
    Secretary for
Army
Army Corps of Engineers (USACE)
Arthritis and Musculoskeletal Interagency
    Coordinating Committee

B

Botanic Garden (USBG)
Broadcasting Board of Governors (BBG) (Voice of
    America, Radio/TV Marti, and more)
Bureau of Alcohol, Tobacco, Firearms, and Explosives
    (ATF)
Bureau of Economic Analysis
Bureau of Engraving and Printing
Bureau of Indian Affairs
Bureau of Industry and Security
Bureau of International Labor Affairs
Bureau of Labor Statistics
Bureau of Land Management
Bureau of Ocean Energy Management
Bureau of Prisons
Bureau of Public Debt
Bureau of Reclamation
Bureau of Safety and Environmental Enforcement
Bureau of the Fiscal Service
Bureau of Transportation Statistics

C

Capitol Police
Census Bureau
Center for Nutrition Policy and Promotion
Centers for Disease Control and Prevention (CDC)
Centers for Medicare & Medicaid Services
Central Intelligence Agency (CIA)
Chemical Safety and Hazard Investigation Board
Citizenship and Immigration Services (USCIS)
Civilian Radioactive Waste Management
Coast Guard (USCG)
Commerce Department
Commission of Fine Arts
Commission on Civil Rights
Commission on International Religious Freedom
Committee for the Implementation of Textile
    Agreements
Community Oriented Policing Services
Community Planning and Development
Compliance, Office of
Comptroller of the Currency, Office of the
Congressional Budget Office
Congressional Research Service
Consular Affairs Bureau
Consumer Financial Protection Bureau
Consumer Product Safety Commission (CPSC)
Cooperative State Research, Education, and
    Extension Service
Copyright Office
Corporation for National and Community Service
Corps of Engineers
Council of Economic Advisers
Council on Environmental Quality
Court of Appeals for the Armed Forces
Court of Appeals for the Federal Circuit
Court of Appeals for Veterans Claims
Court of Federal Claims
Court of International Trade
Court Services and Offender Supervision Agency for
    the District of Columbia
Customs and Border Protection

D

Defense Acquisition University
Defense Advanced Research Projects Agency
Defense Commissary Agency
Defense Contract Audit Agency
Defense Contract Management Agency
Defense Finance and Accounting Service
Defense Information Systems Agency
Defense Intelligence Agency (DIA)
Defense Legal Services Agency
Defense Logistics Agency
Defense Nuclear Facilities Safety Board
Defense Security Cooperation Agency
Defense Security Service
Defense Threat Reduction Agency
Delaware River Basin Commission
Denali Commission
Department of Agriculture (USDA)
Department of Commerce (DOC)
Department of Defense (DOD)
Department of Education (ED)
Department of Energy (DOE)
Department of Health and Human Services (HHS)
Department of Homeland Security (DHS)
Department of Housing and Urban Development (HUD)
Department of the Interior (DOI)
Department of Justice (DOJ)
Department of Labor (DOL)
Department of State (DOS)
Department of Transportation (DOT)
Department of the Treasury
Department of Veterans Affairs (VA)
Director of National Intelligence, Office of
Disability Employment Policy, Office of
Domestic Policy Council
Drug Enforcement Administration (DEA)

E

Economic Adjustment Office
Economic Analysis Bureau
Economic and Statistics Administration
Economic, Business and Agricultural Affairs
Economic Development Administration
Economic Research Service
Election Assistance Commission
Elementary and Secondary Education, Office of
Employee Benefits Security Administration
Employment and Training Administration
Employment Standards Administration

Endangered Species Program
Energy Efficiency and Renewable Energy
Energy Information Administration
English Language Acquisition Office
Environmental Management
Environmental Protection Agency (EPA)
Equal Employment Opportunity Commission (EEOC)
Executive Office for Immigration Review
Export-Import Bank of the United States

F

Fair Housing and Equal Opportunity, Office of
Faith-Based and Community Initiatives Office
Farm Credit System Insurance Corporation
Farm Service Agency (FSA)
Federal Accounting Standards Advisory Board
Federal Aviation Administration
Federal Bureau of Investigation (FBI)
Federal Bureau of Prisons
Federal Communications Commission (FCC)
Federal Deposit Insurance Corporation (FDIC)
Federal Election Commission (FEC)
Federal Emergency Management Agency (FEMA)
Federal Financing Bank
Federal Highway Administration
Federal Home Loan Mortgage Corporation
Federal Housing Administration
Federal Housing Enterprise Oversight
Federal Housing Finance Board
Federal Judicial Center
Federal Labor Relations Authority
Federal Law Enforcement Training Center
Federal Maritime Commission
Federal Mediation and Conciliation Service

Federal Mine Safety and Health Review Commission
Federal Motor Carrier Safety Administration
Federal National Mortgage Association
Federal Protective Service
Federal Railroad Administration
Federal Reserve System
Federal Retirement Thrift Investment Board
Federal Trade Commission (FTC)
Federal Transit Administration
Financial Management Service
Fiscal Responsibility and Reform Commission
Fiscal Service Bureau
Fish and Wildlife Service
Food and Drug Administration (FDA)
Food and Nutrition Service
Food Safety and Inspection Service
Foreign Agricultural Service
Forest Service
Fossil Energy

G

General Services Administration
Geological Survey (USGS)
Global Affairs
Government Accountability Office (GAO)
Government Ethics, Office of
Government National Mortgage Association
Government Publishing Office
Grain Inspection, Packers, and Stockyards
    Administration

H

Health Resources and Services Administration
Healthy Homes and Lead Hazard Control Office
Helsinki Commission
Holocaust Memorial Museum
House of Representatives
House Office of Inspector General
House Office of the Clerk

I

Immigration and Customs Enforcement
Indian Arts and Crafts Board
Indian Health Service
Industrial College of the Armed Forces
Information Resource Management College
Institute of Education Sciences
Institute of Museum and Library Services
Institute of Peace
Inter-American Foundation

Interior Department
Internal Revenue Service (IRS)
International Broadcasting Bureau (IBB)
International Trade Administration (ITA)

J

Job Corps
Joint Chiefs of Staff
Joint Forces Staff College
Joint Military Intelligence College
Joint Program Executive Office for Chemical and
    Biological Defense
Judicial Circuit Courts of Appeal
Judicial Panel on Multidistrict Litigation
Justice Programs, Office of
Juvenile Justice and Delinquency Prevention,
    Office of

L

Labor Department
Labor Statistics, Bureau of
Land Management, Bureau of
Legal Services Corporation
Library of Congress

M

Marine Mammal Commission
Marine Corps
Maritime Administration
Marketing and Regulatory Programs
Marshals Service
Mediation and Conciliation Service
Medicaid
Medicare Payment Advisory Commission
Merit Systems Protection Board
Migratory Bird Conservation Commission
Military Postal Service Agency
Mine Safety and Health Administration
Minority Business Development Agency
Mint
Missile Defense Agency
Mississippi River Commission
Multifamily Housing Office

N

National Aeronautics and Space Administration
    (NASA)
National Agricultural Statistics Service
National AIDS Policy Office
National Archives and Records Administration
    (NARA)

National Capital Planning Commission
National Cemetery Administration
National Council on Disability
National Counterintelligence Executive, Office of
National Credit Union Administration
National Defense University
National Drug Intelligence Center
National Endowment for the Arts
National Endowment for the Humanities
National Flood Insurance Program
National Gallery of Art
National Geospatial-Intelligence Agency
National Guard Bureau
National Highway Traffic Safety Administration
National Indian Gaming Commission
National Institute of Corrections
National Institute of Justice
National Institute of Mental Health
National Institute of Occupational Safety and Health
National Institute of Standards and Technology (NIST)
National Institutes of Health (NIH)
National Labor Relations Board
National Laboratories
National Marine Fisheries
National Mediation Board
National Nuclear Security Administration
National Ocean Service
National Oceanic and Atmospheric Administration (NOAA)
National Park Service
National Science Foundation
National Security Agency
National Security Council
National Technical Information Service
National Telecommunications and Information Administration
National Transportation Safety Board (NTSB)
National War College
National Weather Service
Natural Resources Conservation Service
Navy, Department of the
Nuclear Energy, Science and Technology
Nuclear Regulatory Commission
Nuclear Waste Technical Review Board

O

Occupational Safety & Health Administration (OSHA)
Ocean Energy Management Bureau
Office of Government Ethics
Office of Management and Budget (OMB)
Office of National Drug Control Policy (ONDCP)
Office of Personnel Management
Office of Science and Technology Policy
Office of Special Counsel
Office of Thrift Supervision
Overseas Private Investment Corporation

P

Pacific Northwest Electric Power and Conservation Planning Council
Pardon Attorney Office
Parole Commission
Patent and Trademark Office
Peace Corps
Pension Benefit Guaranty Corporation
Pentagon Force Protection Agency
Pipeline and Hazardous Materials Safety Commission
Policy Development and Research
Political Affairs
Postal Regulatory Commission
Postal Service (USPS)
Postsecondary Education, Office of
Power Administrations
Presidio Trust
Public Diplomacy and Public Affairs
Public and Indian Housing

R

Radio and TV Marti (Español)
Radio Free Asia (RFA)
Radio Free Europe/Radio Liberty (RFE/RL)
Railroad Retirement Board
Reclamation Bureau
Regulatory Information Service Center
Rehabilitation Services Administration
Research and Innovative Technology Administration
Research, Education, and Economics
Risk Management Agency
Rural Business and Cooperative Programs
Rural Development
Rural Housing Service
Rural Utilities Service

S

Safety and Environmental Enforcement Bureau
Saint Lawrence Seaway Development Corporation
Science and Technology Policy Office
Scientific and Technical Information Office
Secret Service
Securities and Exchange Commission (SEC)
Selective Service System
Senate
Small Business Administration (SBA)
Smithsonian Institution
Social Security Administration (SSA)
Social Security Advisory Board
Southeastern Power Administration
Special Education and Rehabilitative Services
State Department
Stennis Center for Public Service
Student Financial Assistance Programs
Substance Abuse and Mental Health Services
    Administration
Supreme Court of the United States
Surface Mining, Reclamation, and Enforcement
Surface Transportation Board
Susquehanna River Basin Commission

T

Tax Court
Taxpayer Advocacy Panel
Taxpayer Advocacy Service
Tennessee Valley Authority
Trade and Development Agency
Transportation Security Administration
Treasury Department
TRICARE Management
Trustee Program

U

U.S. International Trade Commission
U.S. Mission to the United Nations
U.S. National Central Bureau – Interpol
U.S. Trade Representative
Unified Combatant Commands
Uniformed Services University of the Health
    Sciences

V

Veterans Benefits Administration
Veterans Employment and Training Service
Veterans Health Administration
Vietnam Education Foundation
Voice of America (VOA)

W

Weather Service
West Point
Western Area Power Administration
White House
White House Office of Administration
Women's Bureau
Woodrow Wilson International Center for Scholars

Department of Defense Employment Opportunities

The Department of Defense (DOD) is an Executive Department in the U.S. Government. DOD employs over three million military and civilians in three military departments (Army, Navy, and Air Force), the National Guard and various Reserves services, and a number of subordinate agencies. This chart provides information about many of the agencies that employ civilians. After accessing the website, you can find information about employment either by clicking on "careers" or by entering the term "careers" or "employment" in the search bar.

Agency (Acronym)	Approx. # of Staff	Website	Types of Positions
Department of Army	300,000+ civilians	http://www.army.mil Civilian Personnel Sites: http://cpol.army.mil and http://www.armycivilianservice.com	Information technology; communications; audit and finance; security and law enforcement; engineering and science; legal; contracting; logistics and operations management; medical; public affairs; transportation; electrical installation and maintenance; warehousing and stock handling; inventory management; intelligence; international affairs; program managers
Department of Navy	200,000+ civilians	http://www.navy.mil Civilian Personnel Site: http://www.donhr.navy.mil	Information technology; communications; audit and finance; security and law enforcement; engineering and science; legal; contracting; logistics and operations management; medical; public affairs; transportation; electrical installation and maintenance; warehousing and stock handling; inventory management; intelligence; international affairs; program managers
Department of the Air Force	180,000 civilians	http://www.af.mil Civilian Careers: http://www.afciviliancareers.com/	Information technology; communications; audit and finance; security and law enforcement; engineering and science; legal; contracting; logistics and operations management; medical; public affairs; transportation; electrical installation and maintenance; warehousing and stock handling; inventory management; intelligence; international affairs; program managers
Defense Advanced Research Projects Agency (DARPA)	200+	http://www.darpa.mil	Engineering research; adaptive technologies; information innovation; microelectromechanical systems (MEMS), electronics, computing, photonics and biotechnology; strategic technology; tactical technology
Defense Commissary Agency (DeCA)	15,000+	http://www.commissaries.com	Operates more than 250 commissaries worldwide: store workers and clerks; supply technicians, managers; customer service representatives

Agency (Acronym)	Approx. # of Staff	Website	Types of Positions
Defense Contract Audit Agency (DCAA)	5,000+	http://www.dcaa.mil	Finance; auditors; CPAs
Defense Contract Management Agency (DCMA)	10,000+ civilians; 20,000 contractors	http://www.dcma.mil	Contract specialists; contract price analysts; auditors; supply and procurement; acquisition support; property management; software acquisition management; transportation; safety; quality assurance
Defense Finance and Accounting Service (DFAS)	12,000+	http://www.dfas.mil	Accountants; auditors; financial managers; information technology specialists; contract specialists
Defense Information Systems Agency (DISA)	6,000+	http://www.disa.mil	Contract specialists; communications services; information technology specialists; acquisition support; computer scientists; program analysts; operations research analysts; purchasing agents
Defense Intelligence Agency (DIA)	16,500 civilian and military	http://www.dia.mil	Intelligence collection and analysis; radar, acoustic, nuclear, chemical and biological intelligence; information management and information technology; foreign language specialists; program analysts
Defense Logistics Agency (DLA)	27,000 civilian and military	http://www.dla.mil	Supply managers; property disposal specialists; logistics specialists; contract specialists; engineers; information technology specialists, product specialists (quality assurance/ technical)
Defense Security Cooperation Agency (DSCA)	750+ security personnel in regional centers and working with international students	http://dsca.mil	Foreign military sales; strategic planning & integration; information technology; public health advisors; contracting specialists; program analysts; security assistance analysts; financial management analysts; humanitarian assistance program coordinators; FMS analysts
Defense Security Service (DSS)	N/A	http://www.dss.mil/	Counterintelligence; foreign ownership, control or influence (FOCI) professionals; information system security; industrial security; information technology; security education and training (instructor/visual information specialists)
Defense Technical Information Center (DTIC)	N/A	http://www.dtic.mil	Information technology, network security, and database managers; customer service personnel; librarians; technical information specialists; graphic designers; project managers; program and management analysts; web developers; digital preservation specialists; technical writers/editors; marketing specialists; reference and research personnel; trainers

Agency (Acronym)	Approx. # of Staff	Website	Types of Positions
Defense Threat Reduction Agency (DTRA)	2,000	http://www.dtra.mil	Subject Matter Experts on weapons of mass destruction (WMD); physical scientists; engineers; mathematicians; forensics; technology specialists
DOD Education Activity (DODEA)	12,500+ (in 191 schools worldwide)	http://www.dodea.edu	Teachers; instructional specialists; educational aids; school nurses; speech pathologists; school occupational therapists; librarians and library technicians
Missile Defense Agency (MDA)	8,500+	http://www.mda.mil	Engineers; scientists; mathematicians; researchers; computer professionals; information technology specialists; communications specialists; program managers; procurement analysts; contracts management; logistics managers; operations research specialists
National Geospatial-Intelligence Agency (NGA)	14,500+ civilians, military and contractors	https://www1.nga.mil/Careers/Pages/default.aspx	Geospatial intelligence (GEOINT) analysts; imagery scientists; information assurance specialists; project scientists; software, web, and systems engineers; visualization specialists; contract analysts; program managers; counterintelligence officers
National Reconnaissance Office (NRO)	3,000+	http://www.nro.gov	Scientists; engineers; communications specialists; acquisition managers (workforce consists of personnel from DOD, CIA, NGA, NSA, and U.S. Air Force)
Office of Inspector General (DODIG)	1,400	http://www.dodig.mil	Auditors; investigators; special agents; analysts
U.S. Army Corps of Engineers (USACE)	37,000 civilians	http://www.usace.army.mil	Accountants and financial analysts; attorneys; civil works specialists; construction control representatives; contract specialists; engineers; emergency operations specialists; construction managers; disaster response specialists; environmental specialists; logistics specialists; natural resources specialists; park rangers; project managers; real estate managers; research & development personnel; resource management specialists; strategic planners and analysts; trades (e.g., electrician, welding, lock & dam operator, etc.)
Pentagon Force Protection Agency (PFPA)	N/A	http://www.pfpa.mil/	Law enforcement officers (Pentagon Police); criminal investigative and protective agents; threat management agents and technicians; physical security personnel; information technology specialists

Agency (Acronym)	Approx. # of Staff	Website	Types of Positions
Defense Health Agency (DHA)	N/A	http://tricare.mil/tma/default.aspx	Contract and acquisition managers; nurse specialists; physicians; pharmacists; medical technologists; health care scientists; service representatives; conflict resolution professionals; graphic designers; records management; program evaluation and analysis; data management
Washington Headquarters Services	1,200 civilian and military; 2,000 contract employees	http://www.whs.mil	Essential administrative and management services in support of DOD operations including: contracting and procurement; acquisition services; supplies and equipment services; information management; records management; graphics services; budget, financial reporting and analysis; information technology; IT training; risk mitigation; security assessments; telecommunications; safety; environmental management; occupational safety and health; personnel security

In 2004, the Office of the Director of National Intelligence (ODNI) was established to manage the efforts of the Intelligence Community (IC). The work of 17 civilian and military services IC agencies, branches, offices, and bureaus is now consolidated under the ODNI. Each of the organizations within the IC operates under its own directive. This chart provides information about many of the agencies that employ civilians. After accessing the website, you can find information about employment either by clicking on "careers" or entering the term "careers" or "employment" in the search bar.

The Office of Personnel Management's (OPM) Intelligence Series is GS-0132. IC entities typically do not publicly disclose their budget or number of employees.

Information about careers throughout the IC can be found either via USAJOBS (for some but not all of the IC organizations) or at individual entity websites listed below. The website www.intelligence.gov brings together information on career opportunities among the 17 IC agencies across the U.S. and overseas. It is an excellent resource for exploring career choices and applying for positions. Some intelligence agencies offer internships and scholarship opportunities.

Agency (Acronym)	Website	Description / Mission
Office of the Director of National Intelligence	www.odni.gov Careers: http://www.odni.gov/index.php/careers/careers-at-odni	The Director of National Intelligence (DNI) heads up the ODNI and serves as the principal advisor to the President, the National Security Council, and the Homeland Security Council. The ODNI's focus is to promote a more integrated and collaborative IC.
Central Intelligence Agency (CIA)	www.cia.gov Careers: https://www.cia.gov/careers/opportunities	The CIA is separated into four basic components: the National Clandestine Service, the Directorate of Intelligence, the Directorate of Science & Technology, and the Directorate of Support.
Defense Intelligence Agency	www.dia.mil Careers: www.dia.mil/careers.aspx	Department of Defense combat support agency. With more than 16,500 military and civilian employees worldwide, DIA is a major producer and manager of foreign military intelligence and provides military intelligence in support of U.S. military planning and operations and weapon systems acquisition.
Federal Bureau of Investigation (FBI) National Security Branch	www.fbi.gov Careers: https://www.fbijobs.gov/index.asp	Established to combine the missions, capabilities, and resources of the FBI's counterterrorism, counterintelligence, and intelligence elements. The NSB also includes the Terrorist Screening Center, which provides crucial, actionable intelligence to state and local law enforcement, and the High-Value Detainee Interrogation Group, which collects intelligence from key terror suspects to prevent attacks against the U.S. and its allies.

Agency (Acronym)	Website	Description / Mission
National Geospatial-Intelligence Agency (NGA)	www.nga.mil Careers: https://www1.nga.mil/Careers/Pages/default.aspx	Provides timely, relevant, and accurate geospatial intelligence in support of national security objectives. NGA provides support to civilian and military leaders and contributes to the state of readiness of U.S. military forces. NGA also contributes to humanitarian efforts such as tracking floods and fires, and to peacekeeping.
National Reconnaissance Office (NRO)	www.nro.gov Careers: www.nro.gov/careers/careers.html	The NRO's workforce consists of personnel from the DOD, Central Intelligence Agency (CIA), National Geospatial-Intelligence Agency (NGA), and National Security Agency (NSA). The Air Force and CIA comprise the majority of the military and civilian population. Designs, builds, and operates the nation's reconnaissance satellites to warn of potential trouble spots around the world, help plan military operations, and monitor the environment.
National Security Agency Central Security Service	www.nsa.gov Careers: www.nsa.gov/careers	At the forefront of communications and information technology, the nation's cryptologic organization coordinates, directs, and performs highly specialized activities to protect U.S. information systems and to produce foreign signals intelligence information. NSA is also one of the most important centers of foreign language analysis and is said to be the largest employer of mathematicians in the United States and perhaps the world. Its workforce represents an unusual combination of specialties: analysts, engineers, physicists, mathematicians, linguists, computer scientists, researchers, as well as customer relations specialists, security officers, data flow experts, managers, administrative officers, and clerical assistants.
Drug Enforcement Administration (DEA) Office of National Security Intelligence	www.dea.gov Careers: www.dea.gov/careers/occupations.shtml	Enforces the controlled substance laws and regulations of the United States. DEA's Office of National Security Intelligence (ONSI) became a member of the IC in 2006. ONSI facilitates full and appropriate intelligence coordination and information sharing with other members of the U.S. Intelligence Community and homeland security elements. Its goal is to enhance the U.S.'s efforts to reduce the supply of drugs, protect national security, and combat global terrorism.
Department of Energy Office of Intelligence & Counter-Intelligence	www.energy.gov Careers: www.energy.gov/jobs/jobs	Intelligence and counterintelligence activities throughout the DOE complex, including nearly 30 intelligence and counterintelligence offices nationwide.
Department of Homeland Security (DHS) Office of Intelligence & Analysis	www.dhs.gov Careers: www.dhs.gov/careers	Uses information and intelligence from multiple sources to identify and assess current and future threats to the U.S. DHS Intelligence focuses on four strategic areas: promote understanding of threats through intelligence analysis; collect information and intelligence pertinent to homeland security; share information necessary for action; and manage intelligence for the homeland security enterprise.

Agency (Acronym)	Website	Description / Mission
State Department Bureau of Intelligence & Research	www.state.gov Careers: www.state.gov/careers	Provides timely, objective analysis of global developments as well as real-time insights from all-source intelligence. It serves as the focal point within the Department of State for all policy issues and activities involving the Intelligence Community. INR's expert, independent foreign affairs analysts draw on all-source intelligence, diplomatic reporting, INR's public opinion polling, and interaction with U.S. and foreign scholars.
Coast Guard Intelligence	www.uscg.mil Careers: www.uscg.mil/civilian	The Coast Guard's persistent presence in the maritime domain, due to its diverse mission sets and broad legal authorities, allows it to fill a unique niche within the Intelligence Community. Coast Guard Intelligence strives to create decision advantage to advance U.S. interests by providing timely, actionable, and relevant intelligence to shape Coast Guard operations, planning, and decision-making, and to support national and homeland security intelligence requirements.
Air Force Intelligence, Surveillance, & Reconnaissance (AF ISR)	www.af.mil Careers: www.afciviliancareers.com/	The Air Force ISR Agency organizes, trains, equips, and presents forces to conduct intelligence, surveillance, and reconnaissance for combatant commanders and the nation. The AF ISR Agency commander serves as the Service Cryptologic Element under NSA, and oversees Air Force Signals Intelligence activities. The AF ISR Agency has more than 19,000 military and civilian members serving at 72 locations worldwide and commands several subcomponents.
Army Intelligence and Security Command (G-2)	www.army.mil Careers: www.cpol.army.mil	Coordinates the five major military intelligence (MI) disciplines within the Army: Imagery Intelligence, Signals Intelligence, Human Intelligence, Measurement and Signature Intelligence, and Counterintelligence and Security Countermeasures.
U.S. Marine Corps Intelligence Activity	www.hqmc.marines.mil/intelligence Careers: www.hqmc.marines.mil/intelligence/CivilianCareer.aspx	Produces tactical and operational intelligence for battlefield support. Staff expertise includes: geospatial intelligence, advanced geospatial intelligence, signals intelligence, human intelligence, counterintelligence; and ensures there is a single synchronized strategy for the development of the Marine Corps Intelligence, Surveillance, and Reconnaissance Enterprise.
U.S. Navy, Office of Naval Intelligence (ONI)	www.oni.navy.mil Careers: www.oni.navy.mil/Join-Us/Civilian-Careers/Types-of-Jobs/	ONI employs more than 3,000 military, civilian, mobilized reservists, and contractor personnel worldwide, including analysts, scientists, engineers, specialists, and technicians. While ONI is the largest Naval Intelligence organization with the largest concentration of Naval Intelligence civilians, most of Naval Intelligence comprises active duty military personnel, serving throughout the world.

Federal Hiring Charts

Types of Federal Jobs

The charts on these two pages are meant to provide a general overview to help the jobseeker understand a complex landscape. The chart below attempts to capture the most common procedures associated with federal hiring. However, due to numerous regulations, authorities, and exceptions based on unique situations, there may be different hiring scenarios not covered.

Type of Federal Job	Some Features	Where to Find	Hiring Process	Does Veterans' Pref Apply? *	Notes
Competitive Service Jobs	Must follow OPM hiring and personnel rules	USAJOBS or agency websites	Usually competitive: (see page 44); also, Direct Hire and special hiring paths available	**YES for external announcements (open to all U.S. Citizens)** **NO for internal or merit announcements (open to Status Applicants)**	Includes: VEOA, Direct Hire
Excepted Service Jobs	For unique qualification requirements or procedures (i.e., requires a polygraph) Hiring rules may differ	USAJOBS or agency websites	Depends on the agency; various tests; special criteria	Must view job announcement to determine how veterans will be considered	Includes: Pathways, VRA, 30% or more disabled vets, disabled vets enrolled in a training program, Special Appointing Authority for Certain Military Spouses, Schedule A and B, NAF, "Dual Status" Military Technicians
Senior Executive Service	For executive management positions	USAJOBS or agency websites	Competitive application reviewed by Agency Review Board and then Executive Review Board	No	See *The New SES Application 2nd Edition* by Kathryn Troutman and Diane Hudson for more information

*If veterans' preference applies, then:

- Qualified eligible veterans must be considered ahead of non-veterans.

- Compensable disabled veterans can "float" to the top, except for scientific and professional upper-level positions.

- 5 or 10 points are added to veterans' scores when the agency is using the "Rule of Three" hiring process.

Special Federal Hiring Opportunities

This charts summarizes a few of the special federal hiring opportunities available to applicants.

Federal Hiring Path	Some Features	Where to Find	Hiring Process	Does Veterans' Pref Apply?	Notes
Direct Hire [Competitive Service]	Ability to hire quickly for critical needs	USAJOBS, job fairs, or direct contact with hiring managers	Qualified applicant can be hired without the normal competitive hiring process	No	Direct Hire permitted in all agencies for: IT (Infosec), contract specialist, medical officers, nurses, MSWs, pharmacists, Afghanistan reconstruction positions, and positions requiring specific languages
Pathways [Competitive or Excepted Service]	For students and recent graduates	USAJOBS, job fairs, or career centers	Competitive	Yes for competitive service	Internships, Recent Graduate Program, and Presidential Management Fellows (PMF) Programs
"Dual Status" Military Technicians [Excepted Service]	Federal civilian employees who are required to maintain military reserve status as a condition of their employment	USAJOBS	Competitive	Yes	Must be in the military reserves or guard to apply for these positions
NAF [Excepted Service]	Positions on military bases worldwide funded by the activity they serve	USAJOBS and specific DOD agency websites	Competitive, but process depends on organization	Check with the agency policy	May be special conditions, such as living on a military base or required certifications Read the qualifications carefully

See more information about special hiring paths in Step 2
and also on the USAJOBS website at
www.usajobs.gov/Help/working-in-government/unique-hiring-paths/.

Competitive Hiring Process

This chart is a general overview of the competitive hiring process as prescribed by OPM.

See the full process here:
www.opm.gov/policy-data-oversight/human-capital-management/hiring-reform/hiring-process-analysis-tool/

Apply on USAJOBS (Applicant)

- Submit resume and documents
- Answer self-assessment questionnaire

Application Review (HR)

- Check for eiligibility and minimum qualifications
- Rate and rank applicants and apply veterans' preference if appropriate
- Place eligibles in ranking order
- Issue certificate of applicants being referred to the hiring supervisor ("cert list")

Selection (Hiring Manager)

- Select applicants for interview
- Schedule and conduct interviews
- Check references
- Make final selection (congratulations, you have been selected!)

These are some of the major excepted service agencies. All their vacancies may or may not be posted on USAJOBS, so you should view their agency website for additional employment opportunities.

- Federal Reserve System, Board of Governors
- Central Intelligence Agency
- Defense Intelligence Agency
- U.S. Department of State
- Federal Bureau of Investigation
- General Accounting Office
- Agency for International Development
- National Security Agency
- U.S. Nuclear Regulatory Commission
- Postal Rates Commission
- Postal Service
- Tennessee Valley Authority
- U.S. AID
- United States Mission to the United Nations

Department of Veterans Affairs, Health Services and Research Administration:
Physicians, Dentists, Nurses, Nurse Anesthetists, Physicians' Assistants, Podiatrists, Optometrists, Expanded Function Dental Auxiliaries, Occupational Therapists, Pharmacists, Licensed Practical/Vocational Nurses, Physical Therapists, and Certified/Registered Respiratory Therapists.

Judicial Branch

Legislative Branch

Public International Organizations:
- International Monetary Fund
- Pan American Health Organization
- United Nations Children's Fund
- United Nations Development Program
- United Nations Institute
- United Nations Population Fund
- United Nations Secretariat
- World Bank, International Finance Corporation (IFC), and the Multilateral Investment Guarantee Agency (MIGA)

Find a link to the list of excepted service agencies and excepted service positions at:
www.resume-place.com/resources/useful-links/

Non-appropriated Funds (NAF) Federal Jobs

NAF jobs are federal jobs located on military bases worldwide, but they are different from federal civil service employment, because the monies used to pay the salaries of NAF employees come from a different source. Civil service positions are paid for by money appropriated by Congress. NAF employee are paid from non-appropriated funds of Army and Air Force Exchange Service, Navy Exchange Service Command, Marine Corps exchanges, or any other armed forces organization for the comfort, pleasure, contentment, or physical or mental improvement of members of the armed forces. Benefits are great!

Army:
www.USAJOBS.gov
Search: "NAF Army"

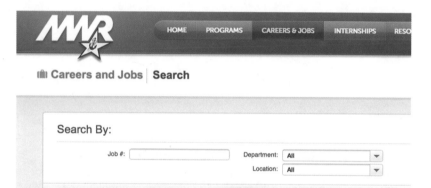

Navy:
www.navymwr.org/jobs/
and USAJOBS
On USAJOBS, search: "NAF Navy"

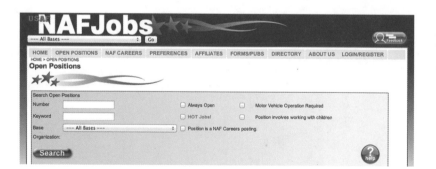

Air Force:
www.nafjobs.org/viewjobs.aspx
On USAJOBS, search "NAF Air Force"

Marine Corps:
www.usmc-mccs.org/careers/ (click on Prospective Employees under Job Search & Apply)
On USAJOBS, search "NAF USMC"

Who Can Receive NAF Employment Benefits?

NAF positions are classified as either "flexible" or "regular." Flexible employees have work schedules that depend on the needs of the activity. These employees may work a minimum of zero hours to a maximum of 40 hours per week, and do not receive benefits. Regular employees work between 20 and 40 hours a week depending on position requirements, and are entitled to receive benefits.

Employee Benefits Available to All Regular Full-Time and Regular Part-Time Civilian NAF Employees:

Medical and Dental
Life Insurance
Optional and Dependent Life Insurance
Accidental Death and Dismemberment
401(k) Savings Plan
Group Retirement Plan
Family Friendly Leave Program
Flexible Spending Account
Long-Term Care
Short-Term Disability
Leave (Sick & Vacation)

Benefits and Privileges

All NAF employees are encouraged to enjoy the use of NAF facilities and take advantage of a variety of employee benefits. (Facilities do vary from base to base.) Facilities include:

Exchanges
Lodging & Dining Clubs
Childcare Facilities
Movie Theaters & Parks
Swimming Pools & Fitness Centers
Golf Courses
Bowling Centers
Marinas & Ocean Fishing
Libraries
Hobby Shops
Discount Tickets to your favorite places and Leisure Travel Deals
Flexible Schedules
Training Opportunities
Tuition Assistance at applicable commands
Balance of Work & Family Life
Employee Assistance Program (EAP)
Paid Holidays
Financial Wellness Program
All of this in a secure, fast paced, professional, family oriented, working environment.

For Employees and Retirees

The DOD implemented the Health Benefits Program (HBP) on January 1, 2000. It provides comprehensive benefits which include hospitalization, prescription drugs, medical, surgical, preventive, mental health, substance abuse, vision, and dental care.

The HBP, through Aetna, provides access to in-network doctors, hospitals, health care facilities, and pharmacies, globally, along with claims administration services for the HBP. Aetna, as the Third Party Administrator, processes and pays medical and dental claims. Premiums from participants collected through payroll deductions on a bi-weekly basis. More information about the benefit can be found at Aetna.com and/or Aetna.Navigator.

U.S. Army MWR NAF Position Benefits: http://www.armymwr.com/naf-benefits.aspx
U.S. Navy Sample NAF Resume: http://www.navymwr.org/assets/home/docs/sampleResumeFormat.pdf

STEP

2

Network—Who Do You Know?

NETWORKING CAN LAND YOU A FEDERAL JOB!

Networking is a great opportunity to learn about the federal hiring system. Other people, especially current and former federal employees, are often the best source of basic information and insider tips.

Do you know a supervisor at an agency or a military base? It's possible that veterans could get hired by this supervisor. The Veterans' Recruitment Appointment (VRA) offers special hiring programs for retiring and separating military (disabled or non-disabled). VRA gives supervisors the authority to make direct hires in the case of veterans. Find out about other networking job opportunities in this step.

Photo: Kathryn Troutman and ACS Schofield Barracks staff at the Hiring Our Heroes Summit, U.S. Chamber of Commerce, Wheeler AFB, Oahu, Hawaii, October 2016 – Transitioning military and spouses are in line for the Job Fair and Summit!

One of the best places to learn about federal jobs, agencies, and opportunities is at a military career expo. On occasion, the federal human resources specialist may even bring along a few Direct Hire opportunities for government positions or internships. Have your resume ready to hand out. Your federal resume should feature your most relevant skills for easy reading and review by the human resources recruiters. Also, practice the job fair script before you go.

Job Fair Script

Prepare your own job fair script here. Practice your script with a friend.

Hello, my name is: _____

Where are you from? _____

Military service: _____
_____

Recent activity: _____
What was involved in that? _____
What was the result of that activity? _____
What was your role? _____

What kind of job are you looking for? _____
_____
_____

What are your basic skills? _____
_____
_____

Where do you want to live now? _____

If you are eligible for a Special Hiring Authority listed on pages 52 - 53, you can contact a Veteran Employment Program Manager, Selective Placement Coordinator, Hiring Manager, or human resources specialist DIRECTLY, to discuss your eligibility and possible non-competitive consideration for positions before they are advertised on USAJOBS.

Networking Contacts

Selective Placement Program Coordinators

If you are a 30% or more disabled veteran, or a person with a targeted disability, you could network with Selective Placement Program Coordinators to inquire about opportunities for being hired non-competitively.

www.opm.gov/policy-data-oversight/disability-employment/
selective-placement-program-coordinator-directory/

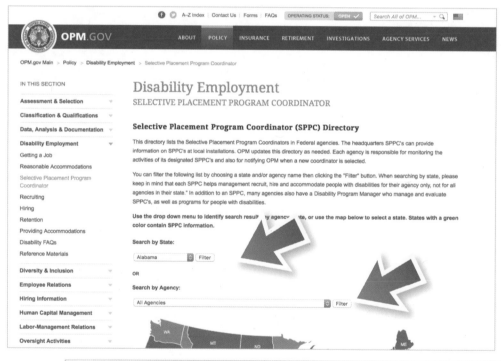

Write to these HR Disability Specialists

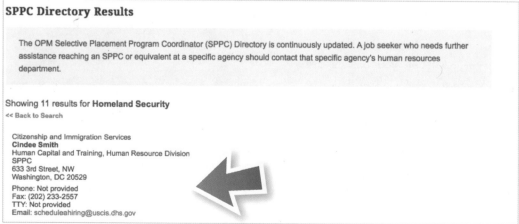

Veterans' Representatives

If you are a veteran, you can network with agency Veterans' Representatives directly to find out if there are opportunities for being hired non-competitively.

www.fedshirevets.gov/AgencyDirectory/index.aspx

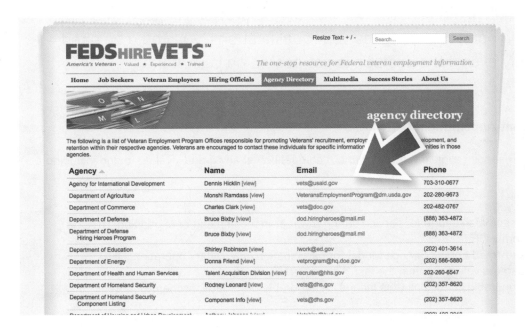

Write to these Veterans' Representatives directly! Include your resume, cover letter, and DD-214, Statement of Service and/or VA letter.

Hiring Managers and Human Resources Specialists

If you are a candidate for any of the Special Hiring Authorities below, you can contact a Hiring Manager or an HR specialist DIRECTLY (or talk to them at a job fair) about non-competitive federal positions that may not be advertised on USAJOBS. They could use your special hiring program to consider you for a federal position.

Networking Ideas

- **Job Expo:** Take your two-page networking resume (samples on pages 54 to 57.)
  Also take your supporting documentation for the agency representative or recruiter.

- **Email:** Send your introductory cover letter, federal resume and appropriate documentation to the Veterans' Representatives, Selective Placement Program Coordinator or HR specialist to introduce your skills and interest in a position at their agency.

- **LinkedIn:** Research specific agency managers or human resources specialists and write to them through LinkedIn, to see if you can write to them directly regarding a federal position using one of the Special Hiring Authorities.

- **Cover Letter:** Send a customized cover letter that will specify the types of positions that you are seeking and your salary or grade level locations. See a cover letter sample in Step 7, pages 138-139.

- **Follow-up is critical!** If you do not hear from them, be sure to follow up.

Special Hiring Programs and Authorities

NETWORKING TIP: If you are eligible for one of these special hiring programs and authorities, you could get hired for a federal position by contacting someone in the non-competitive hiring network listed on the previous page. If they have or know of a position open that matches your qualifications, you could be hired non-competitively even if the position is not posted on USAJOBS.

Veterans' Recruitment Appointment (VRA)

VRA allows agencies to appoint eligible veterans without competition at any grade level up to and including a GS-11 or equivalent.

You are VRA eligible if you:
- are in receipt of a campaign badge for service during a war or in a campaign or expedition, OR
- are a disabled veteran, OR
- are in receipt of an Armed Forces Service Medal for participation in a military operation, OR
- are a recently separated veteran (within the last 3 years), AND
- separated under honorable conditions (this means an honorable or general discharge).

After successfully completing two years, you will be converted to the competitive service. Agencies can also use VRA to fill temporary or term positions, but in these cases you will not be converted to the competitive service after two years. Veterans' preference applies when using the VRA authority. There is no limit to the number of times you can apply under VRA.

You must provide acceptable documentation of your preference or appointment eligibility. The Member 4 Copy of your DD-214, "Certificate of Release or Discharge from Active Duty," is preferable. If claiming 10-point preference, you will need to submit a Standard Form (SF-15), "Application for 10-Point Veteran Preference."

30% or More Disabled Veteran

You may be eligible as a 30% or more disabled veteran if you are:
- Retired from active military service with a disability rating of 30% or more; or
- Received a rating from the Department of Veterans Affairs (VA) dated 1991 or later to include disability determinations from a branch of the Armed Forces at any time, as having a compensable service-connected disability of 30% or more.

Learn more at www.opm.gov/policy-data-oversight/veterans-employment-initiative/vet-guide/#30%Disabled.

You must provide a copy of your DD-214 (Member 4 Copy), VA letter that shows your disability percentage, and a completed SF-15 Application for 10-point veterans preference.

Persons with Disabilities (Schedule A)

You may be eligible as a Person with Disability if you are:

- An individual with an intellectual disability, a severe physical disability, or a psychiatric disability which has been certified by a licensed medical professional, vocational rehabilitation specialist or any other federal, state, or District of Columbia agency that issues or provides disability benefits.

Learn more at www.opm.gov/policy-data-oversight/disability-employment/hiring/.

You must provide a copy of the letter documenting your disability from a licensed professional.

Certain Former Overseas Federal Employees under Executive Order 12721

You may be eligible under Executive Order 12721 if you:

- Worked overseas as an appropriated fund federal employee while a family member of a civilian, non-appropriated fund, or uniformed service member serving overseas, for an accumulated total of 52 weeks and received a fully successful (pass) or better performance appraisal. This appointment eligibility is effective for a period of three years following the date of return from overseas to the United States to reassume residence.

Learn more about eligibility requirements at http://www.presidency.ucsb.edu/ws/?pid=23562.

You must provide a copy of a recent SF-50 Notification of Personnel Action to support your claim, and a copy of your most recent performance appraisal. Ask your supervisor or HR department for these documents.

Military Spouse under Executive Order 13473

You may be eligible under Executive Order 13473 if you are:

- A spouse of a member of the armed forces serving on active duty who has orders specifying a permanent change of station (not for training); or
- A spouse of a 100 percent disabled service member injured while on active duty; or
- An un-remarried widow or widower of a service member who was killed while performing active duty.

The National Defense Authorization Act (NDAA) for Fiscal Year 2017 removes the two-year limit for military spouses referenced in the EO 13473.

Spouses eligible based on a permanent change of duty station are limited to the geographic area as specified in the permanent change of station orders. This includes the surrounding area which people reasonably can be expected to travel daily to and from work.

Learn more about the Noncompetitive Appointment of Certain Military Spouses at FedsHireVets https://www.fedshirevets.gov/hire/hrp/qaspouse/ or view the full text at https://www.federalregister.gov/documents/2011/08/31/2011-22268/noncompetitive-appointment-of-certain-military-spouses.

DAN LOW
1234 Murphy Lane | Philadelphia, PA 19104
(555) 123-4567 | danlow@yahoo.com

Career Objective: Special Agent / Investigations / 1811 Positions
Citizenship: United States
Veterans' Preference: 30% or more disabled, E-5, USMC 2006-2012, Purple Heart Recipient
Clearance: Active Department of Defense SECRET Security Clearance
Languages: Korean and English

EDUCATION

BACHELOR OF SCIENCE, Rosemont College · Rosemont, PA · May 2015
Major: Criminal Justice · GPA: 3.70

ASSOCIATE OF SCIENCE, Delaware County Community College · Media, PA · June 2013
Major: Criminal Justice · GPA: 3.60 · Phi Theta Kappa Honors

PROFESSIONAL EXPERIENCE

General Supply Specialist (GS-2001-07)   **08/2015 – Present**
Department of Veterans Affairs, Philadelphia, PA 19104   Salary: $34,079/year
Supervisor: Frank Jackson, 987-654-0123, may contact   40+ Hours per Week

Pathways to Career Excellence (PaCE) Program participant performing progressively more responsible assignments as a General Supply Specialist for the Defense Logistics Agency (DLA).

PLANNING AND ORGANIZATION: Demonstrate knowledge of technical supply principles, concepts and methodologies including inventory, packaging, storing, distribution and cataloging. Plan and prepare for annual inventory; participate in inventory process and random audits, special audits, inspections and studies, individually and as part of a team; check property records to investigate causes of discrepancies.

ORAL COMMUNICATION: Respond to internal and external questions from ICP/Supply Center and customers relative to shipment status and expediting material. Resolve problems and trace shipments upon request. Communicate professionally with all inquirers, maintaining a calm, pleasant demeanor even in stressful conditions.

EVALUATING INFORMATION: Review and analyze results of all audits. Analyze processes, materials and documentation to establish accuracy and effectiveness of operations, and to identify deficiencies or trends affecting quality of the service/product provided to the customer. Perform extensive and exhaustive searches to compile, organize and assess data related to transportation, material and location errors in order to identify unfavorable trends and potential causes of discrepancies. Compile results of analyses; prepare written reports; brief operating officials and management on findings and make recommendations for corrective actions and potential solutions. Develop and implement follow-up procedures to assess effectiveness of improvement actions taken.

PRIORITIZING, ADAPTABILITY AND FLEXIBILITY: Arrange routes to handle shipments with urgent delivery dates, or shipments to destinations that are isolated or cannot be transported through normal channels. Reschedule shipments based on priority and available equipment.

Claims Assistant (GS-0996-07)   **02/2015 – 08/2015**
Department of Veterans Affairs, Philadelphia, PA 19104   Salary: $34,079/year
Supervisor: Frank Jackson, 987-654-0123, may contact   40+ Hours per Week

EVALUATING INFORMATION AND DECISION MAKING: Examined applications for benefits. Evaluated information and applied rules and processes concerning claims. Reviewed offers of settlements; advised claimants regarding acceptance or rejection of offers. Compared and evaluated information on claims and supporting documentation.

Introducing Dan Low: Separated as 30% or more disabled veteran (CPS) as USMC Rifleman; got a BS in criminology on the GI Bill; worked as IRS intern and now as a DLA Pathways participant to prepare for Special Agent position.

Returned incomplete applications and requested additional information. Applied rules, regulations and techniques regarding dependents; rendered determinations and annual reviews for dependents eligible for basic allowances.

ORGANIZING AND PLANNING: Assisted specialists and other legal employees in planning strategy to present the Government in its most favorable position by citing State and Federal Laws, including contractual laws governing each functional case. Consolidated files and related folders. Assisted probation officers or their designees, as needed, in finalizing payment plans.

ORAL AND WRITTEN COMMUNICATION: Counseled complainants on options for recourse under the garnishment law. Coordinated with guards and Federal police in protecting the building and responding to incidents. Advised personnel on job expectations. Prepared correspondence with claimants and other parties involved in claims process.

Security Assistant (Intern)   10/2013 – 11/2014
Internal Revenue Service, Philadelphia, PA 19104   Salary: Volunteer
Supervisor: Michael Hoffman, 987-654-3210, may contact   25 Hours per Week

PHYSICAL SECURITY: Applied a practical knowledge of security procedures, processes, and techniques in performing a variety of security duties in support of protecting a Level 4 security building. Conducted surveillance and foot patrols. Controlled the movement of persons around and in the building. Conducted investigations of incidents and prepared required reports.

ORAL COMMUNICATION: Briefed employees and visitors on controls and restrictions related to building access. Conducted training and PowerPoint presentations concerning security issues and restrictions. Coordinated with guards and Federal police in protecting the building and responding to incidents.

Rifleman   09/2006 – 07/2012
Marine Corps, 2nd Battalion   Rank: Lance Corporal
Kaneohe Bay, HI · Baghdad, Iraq   Salary: $45,000/ year
Supervisor: Capt. Thomas Jefferson (123-456-7890)   40+ Hours per Week

Deployed to the Haditha Triad, Iraq, in support of Operation Iraqi Freedom.

LEADERSHIP, ORGANIZATION AND PLANNING: Supervised and motivated Marines in combat. Led a 4-soldier team on mounted patrols. Organized and planned security around Iraqi checkpoints to search vehicles for weapons.

COMMUNICATION AND INTERPERSONAL SKILLS: Part of a team that led a rigorous training program to teach Iraqi police personnel how to use U.S. weapons and tactics. Interacted with civilians, promoting cooperation and good will.

SECURITY MANAGEMENT: Provided security for high-profile meetings between the platoon commander and Iraqi sheikhs. Provided foot and mobilized patrols of control points and the forward operating base to provide front line security. Transported convicted Marines to military jail and military trials.

SEARCH OPERATIONS: Conducted patrols and searches for high value target terrorists and IEDs in dangerous areas of the town. Conducted house searches based on intelligence and detained known or suspected terrorists. Demonstrated INITIATIVE AND MOTIVATION in conducting patrols and searches.

Accomplishments: Awarded the Purple Heart for being wounded in a firefight while posting security for a Marine to cross a long open field. Awarded Combat Action Ribbon for participation under enemy fire in ground combat firefight.

TRAINING & CERTIFICATIONS
First Aid and CPR/AED, American Red Cross, 12/2014 · Military Academic Skills Program, 11/2008 · Marine Rifleman: Combat Skills, 9/2007 · Land Navigation, 9/2007 · Combat Water Surface Survival, USMC, 8/2007 · Advanced Aircraft Ditching, USMC, 8/2007 · IPHABD Qualification, USMC, 8/2007 · Basic Aircraft Ditching, USMC, 8/2007 · Surface Survival, USMC, 8/2007 · Infantry Patrolling, 7/2007 · Fundamentals of Marine Corps Leadership, 6/2006 · Infantry School, 3/2006 · Marine Recruit Training Boot Camp, 09/2005

ANESHA T. GAFFNEY

PSC 999 Box 11, Rota, Spain, FPO, AE, 09634
666.666.6666
Email: anesha.gaffney@yahoo.com

Family Member of USN Active Duty
Eligible for Consideration under Executive Order 13473, September 11, 2009

SUMMARY OF SKILLS:
Instructor, Adult Educator
Program Developer and Coordinator
Mentor and Coach, Community Liaison
Administration, Writing and Computer Skills
Public Speaker and Speaking Coach

HIGHLIGHTS OF EXPERIENCE:

- **Family readiness and quality of life support:** career advisor, relocation counselor, and referrals for needed services for USN family members in Rota.

- **Provided adult education, instruction, and training** at University of West Florida, and increased operational readiness.

- **Coordinated and supervised** first Annual Northwest Florida Districts High School Speech Tournament.

- **Community liaison** establishing a network for the University of West Florida and N.A.S. Pensacola.

- **President's Award for Leadership and Diversity**, Univ. of W. FL (2008).

- **Proficient in Microsoft Office programs,** Windows Movie Maker, Final Cut Pro, and iMovie. **Typing Speed 60 wpm.**

WORK EXPERIENCE:

Fleet and Family Support Center, US Navy, Rota, Spain
Volunteer, 8/2015 – Present, 20 hours per week

INFORMATION AND REFERRAL: Identified and clarified issues or concerns and determined appropriate referral services for military members, retirees, and family members. Ensured customer service and satisfaction.

CUSTOMER SERVICE: Primary contact for department and ensured and delivered services to customers including educating clients on Relocation Services and Career Resource Development.

MARKETING: Gathered data for Fleet and Family Support Center and updated information for department calendar and for NAVSTA Rota advertisement.

DATA GATHERING: Utilized Microsoft Office software to compile and report information and statistics for use at the installation.

University of West Florida, Tampa, FL
Graduate Assistant Coach, 8/2012 to 6/2015, 30 hours per week

INSTRUCTOR AND COACH. Designed training structure and determined appropriate alternative routes to more effective coaching techniques.

-- Over 5,000 hours of coaching students in effective writing and presentation skills.

RECRUITER. Made recommendations for University of West Florida Forensics Team. Community liaison for team.

-- Created promotional DVDs; coordinated external events on campus to recruit on-campus students. Coordinated with Director of Forensics with national and regional travel plans for approximately 10 students.

EDUCATION:

Master of Science, Public Administration, 2015
University of West Florida, Pensacola, FL
Financial Management, Public Budgeting
Public Service Human Resources Management
Conflict Management & Resolution, Marketing Management

Bachelor of Arts in Organizational Communications, 2012
University of West Florida, Pensacola, FL
- Leadership Communications (Project Car-A-Van) - raised funds to purchase 15-passenger van for Ronald McDonald House of Northwest Florida (2011).
- Health Communications (Project KidCare) - Worked with Florida KidCare to raise awareness of medical insurance to families of lower socioeconomic status (2011).

HONORS:

- Outstanding Graduate Student Award, University of West Florida (2015) Recipient of Letter of Appreciation from Commanding Officer for Volunteer Service, N.A.S. Pensacola (2011)
- President's Award for Leadership and Diversity, Univ. of West Florida (2012)
- Four-time National Finalist: 2012 Pi Kappa Delta National Speech and Debate Championship Finalist (2009-2012)
- Top 24 collegiate speaker in the US in multiple categories, National Forensic Association (2012)
- Volunteer Shining Star Award, Ronald McDonald House of Northwest Florida (2011)

LinkedIn Networking

Life is about relationships, and LinkedIn has opened the door to help build more relationships worldwide.

LinkedIn, with 250 million professionals in its network, is THE business channel for recruiting.

However, it is also so much more. LinkedIn provides an opportunity to build a worldwide network of professionals who can assist you with your career. Not only does it work for military to civilian transitions, it also works within the military framework where military to military assignments are concerned. Many military members have made connections for their next military assignment with another military professional using LinkedIn. LinkedIn can be regarded as a marvelous "networking" tool, though it should not be used as a substitute for good old-fashioned relationship building.

LinkedIn is a great tool for military spouses for PCS moves.

Before LinkedIn, it was very difficult to build a professional network outside of your current assignment. With the worldwide network that LinkedIn provides, military spouses are now able to build a professional network online.

Whether it is a short notice PCS move, a change in PCS orders, or a normal PCS rotation, or even in the case of a service member's extended or remote tours of duty (deployment etc.), military spouses can build strong professional networks via LinkedIn.

Fast updates to your network (and their network) for frequent moves!

With the ability of LinkedIn to share the same message with 50 of your contacts at a click of the button, it will not take long to inform your entire contact list of any changes in your business and professional circumstance. Each of your contacts will also have other contacts who will be able to refer you to positions, whether you are simply looking for a change or moving due to a military assignment.

Employers expect to find professionals on LinkedIn.

Many of our clients report that their LinkedIn profile was reviewed prior to their interview by the interviewers. This situation works fabulously both ways. The interviewer will have a great impression of you if you have done your work on LinkedIn, and you can research the interviewer prior to your interview.

The LinkedIn resume for Natalie Richardson on the facing page was developed based on her federal resume.

We added an exciting profile with her most outstanding skills. LinkedIn is a professional place where you can post a photograph and introduce your strengths, mission, and career history to an employer or network. You can even ask for recommendations from your best customers or team members who will write about your strengths and accomplishments.

Did You Know?

Business professionals and human resources managers use LinkedIn to check out potential job candidates. Individuals with more than 20 connections are **34 times** more likely to be approached with a job opportunity.

Natalie Richardson

2nd

Public Affairs Specialist at US Navy Reserves

Chesapeake, Virginia | Public Relations and Communications

| Previous | Sendmilitarycoupons.com, Self-Promotions Biz Cards, Chiropractic Health-Care |
| Education | Devry University-California |

Connect | **Send Natalie InMail** ▾

2
connections

www.linkedin.com/in/nbrichardson

Background

Summary

Is your company looking for a Public Relations Specialist experienced in Military Affairs? Do you need somebody who can shape the message of your organization to reach new audiences? I am your public affairs specialist!

"Send It To Your Sweetie" Program took off! I founded and ran a successful marketing program for military families who had loved ones in Iraq. This unique program offered free services to military families with members in Iraq for shipping, phone messages, and personal delivery of gifts for their loved ones. I also liaised with base command to ensure all regulations and policies were met.

My expertise includes:
- Entrepreneurial spirit and creativity
- Communications and liaison
- Writing and marketing strategies
- Community relations
- Caring for military families and veterans

Employers search LinkedIn by zip code, which is automatically tied to your city and state.

Moving? Put your NEW location into your LinkedIn account.

Experience

Public Affairs Specialist

US Navy Reserves

February 2012 – Present (2 years 3 months) | Hampton, Virginia Area

Successfully landed excellent position as GS-9 Public Affairs Specialist in charge of all advertising for recruiting program.

PARTNER/MANAGER

Sendmilitarycoupons.com

September 2010 – February 2011 (6 months) | San Diego, CA

MARKETING PROGRAM FOR MILITARY FAMILIES WITH FAMILY MEMBER IN IRAQ. Developed, owned, managed and operated business that sold marketing contracts to local businesses. Marketed "Send It To Your Sweetie" program targeting free services to military families with members in Iraq for shipping, phone messages, and personal delivery of gifts for their loved ones. Met with base command to ensure all regulations and policies were met.

• Accomplishment: Conceptualized a successful program for family members to send gifts and messages to military personnel. More than 2,500 messages were sent through this program in just 6 months. Sold business in less than 6 months for a substantial profit.

COMMUNICATIONS. Wrote business plan and developed all aspects of advertising and marketing. Performed cold calls on business customers and followed up with written proposals. Created and delivered PowerPoint presentations to groups of various sizes. Organized and prepared mailings to families and businesses.

WEBSITE DESIGN: Designed website and prepared spreadsheet to track monthly views and clicks. Due to volume of business, interviewed and hired 3 contractors to assist with billing, designing ads, and updating website.

MANAGER

Self-Promotions Biz Cards

June 2005 – July 2009 (4 years 2 months) | 29 Palms, CA

CREATIVE PRODUCTION: Sold and created full-color, personalized business cards to small businesses. Planned and organized work; efficiently and effectively processed the sale, design, ordering and delivery of product. Ensured quality control and timeliness for re-orders.

• Established a successful in-home business with local producers of business cards. Contracted with more than 15 vendors and tracked orders for more than 200 customers in two years. Efficiently set up and managed own schedule and schedule for automatic reordering.

CUSTOMER SERVICES: Provided administrative support to customers and vendors. Prepared and sent invoices, collected. Conducted all aspects of accounting.

COMMUNICATION: Corresponded with clients by email and phone, ensured correct grammar, spelling and format. Made cold calls on small businesses – utilized interpersonal skills to develop customer base of 300 businesses within 6 months.

COMPUTER SKILLS: Utilized typing speed of 45 wpm, Microsoft Suite programs for reports and communication, as well as Photoshop, Illustrator and Corel software to design cards.

Demonstrated strong customer services skills; multi-tasked and worked under pressure and constant deadlines. Maintained customer relations; photographed clients and worked with customers to achieve their desired customized product.

PUBLIC RELATIONS

Chiropractic Health-Care

February 2004 – January 2005 (1 year) | San Diego, CA

BUSINESS DEVELOPMENT AND COMMUNICATIONS: Represented chiropractic clinic public relations, made new business contacts, mended old contacts. Developed lasting business relationships with store managers, district managers and their assistants both inside and outside the office. Scheduled health screenings involving blood pressure, glucose and cholesterol testing. Ensured excellent service. Successfully increased patient roster by an average of 5 new patients per week.

STORE MANAGER

Lulu's Boutique

April 2002 – February 2004 (1 year 11 months) | Los Angeles, CA

ADMINISTRATION: Performed office and store administration including management of files and official records, training, payroll and reporting. Communicated effectively orally and in writing. Developed, wrote, standardized and regulated customer service procedures, policies and systems.

COMMUNICATIONS: Communicated with diverse customers, vendors, management to increase sales and resolve problems. Greeted and assisted customers with special requests. Trained staff to deliver excellent customer service.

COMPUTER SKILLS: Utilized computer skills to design website and regulate maintenance for user effectiveness. Used Microsoft Word for correspondence and Excel for reports. Ensured accuracy, correct grammar, spelling, punctuation and syntax.

MANAGED STAFF AND BUDGET: Planned and organized work for sales staff; managed budgeting for cost effective sales planning, directed all tasks and aspects of controlling, maintaining and rotating inventory. Designed store layout and product presentations.

MARKETING SOLUTIONS: Gathered pertinent data, and recognized solutions to initiate and conduct successful storewide marketing campaigns. Controlled and minimized expenses to maximize profit through selected business improvements.

 Languages

Spanish   **French**

 Skills & Endorsements

Microsoft Office

Spanish

French

Graphic Design

 Education

Devry University-California

2000 – 2002

Activities and Societies: Marketing and Business Courses

STEP

Research Vacancy Announcements on USAJOBS

The best way to begin writing a Best Qualified federal resume is to FIRST find a USAJOBS announcement that matches your qualifications.

Photo: Kathryn Troutman teaching Ten Steps to a Federal Job® at Schofield Barracks, Army Community Services, Oct. 2016

Follow the Directions!

The following items are the most important elements of a vacancy announcement. Be sure to study these items on every announcement so that you follow the directions successfully.

Closing Date: The closing dates are getting closer!

Due to the number of applications, many closing dates are getting shorter even to just 1-2 days. Get your federal resume written in advance so that you are ready to apply when you find the perfect USAJOBS announcement. If an announcement reads "Open Continously" or "Inventory Building," or has a closing date that is 12 months away, then this announcement is a database-building announcement. Submit your application at least one day early in case there is a complication with the submission. NOTE: Disabled veterans CAN apply to positions after the closing date, but it is better to submit on time.

Who May Apply

Read this section first to see if you can apply for the position. Some announcements very specific and only open to curent employees of that agency in a specific location.

Duties

The description of duties will be written based on the actual position description. The write-up will include "keywords" that should be included in a federal resume.

Qualifications

Are you qualified? Read the qualifications to determine if you have the general and specialized qualifications. If the announcement states one year, that means 52 weeks, 40 hours per week.

Knowledge, Skills, and Abilities are KEYWORDS!

If KSAs are listed in the announcement, you will need to cover them in the federal resume. Follow the Outline Format federal resume examples featured in this book with the KSAs for headlines in your work experience descriptions. Then add an accomplishment that will demonstrate your KSAs.

How to Apply

Carefully read the "how to apply" instructions as they will differ from agency to agency.

The usual application includes a resume, KSAs (if requested separately), last performance evaluation (if possible), DD-214 (if you were in the military), and transcripts (if requested or if you are applying based on education).

Questionnaires: Beware, this is a TEST! You need to score 85 to 90!

In the "Self-Assessment Questionnaires" you rate your own skill and experience. Do not deflate your answers. Give yourself all the credit that you can. Your Questionnaire score typical would need to be at least 85% or higher in order to get Best Qualified. PLUS ... Your resume must match your answers to the questions. Human Resources will compare the Questionnaire to your resume.

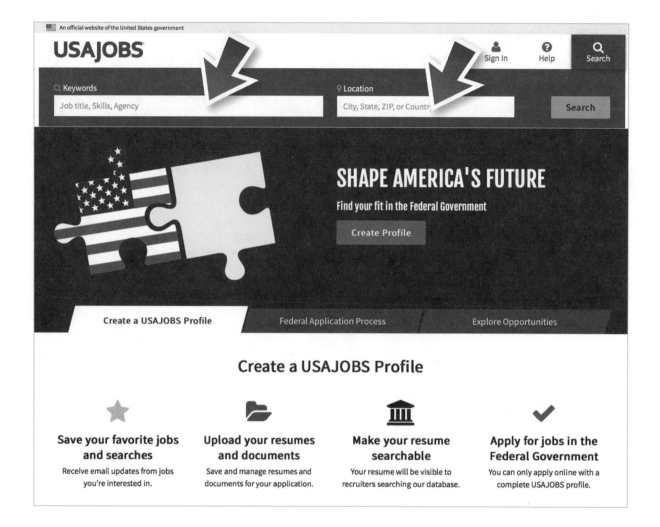

Basic Search: Keyword and Geographic Location

The Basic Search is VERY EASY: Keyword/Job Title and Geographic Location. This is the easiest search to perform and will return a large number of results.

- Go to the USAJOBS home page.
- Enter keywords and geographic location.
- Try to use keywords specific to your unique skill set or the correct job title in quotation marks.

Other USAJOBS Search Options:
Search for <u>All U.S. Citizens</u> positions in Washington, DC (1315 jobs)

Search for <u>Federal Employees</u> positions in Washington, DC (2713 jobs)
Notice that the number of "Federal Employee" announcements is double that of U.S. Citizen announcements!

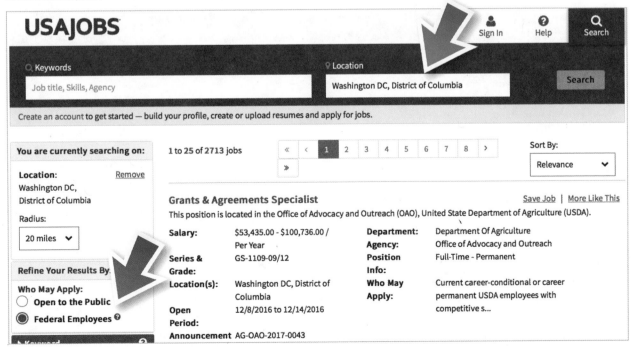

Search for "Title 32" positions (National Guard or Reserve Membership Required)

Tip: Search phrases with quotes for more accuracy

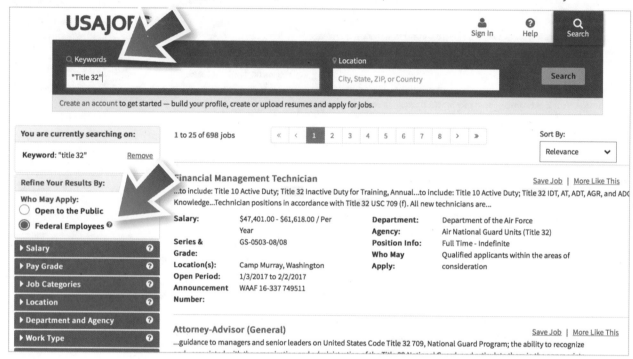

Search for "Direct Hire" positions in Washington, DC (can be filled quickly!)

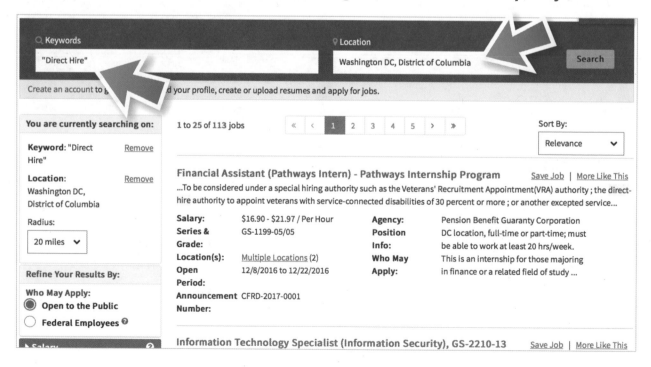

Search for "Excepted Service" positions in Washington, DC

Search for "Army NAF" positions open to all U.S. citizens

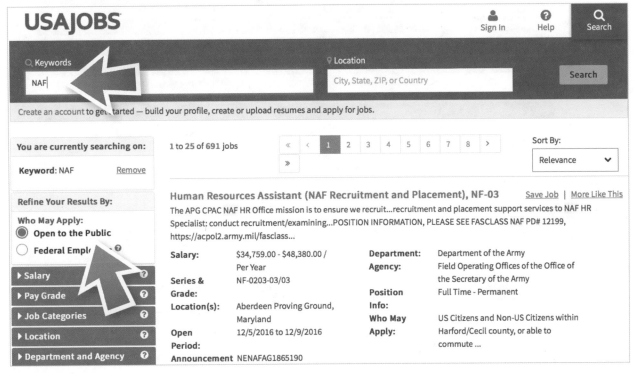

USAJOBS Advanced Search

You can quickly and efficiently refine your USAJOBS job announcement search using the Advanced Search function.

Tip: If you specify too many criteria, you will have fewer results. I recommend including Occupational Series, Grade, and Geographic Location.

For the above question "Who May Apply":
- If you are a veteran, Schedule A, or any of the choices above, answer YES.
- If you have no special hiring program consideration, answer NO.

You can save your favorite searches and even get convenient, regular emails with updated postings.

We searched below on "IT Specialist" positions in California in the GS-09 to 11 range.

Save this search by clicking on this button

Name your search carefully

Save this search

Name Your Saved Search   *Required*

IT Specialist Gs 9 - 11 California

Sort Results By

Relevance ⌄

How often do you want to receive email notifications to your primary email address? ❓
◉ Daily   ○ Weekly   ○ Monthly   ○ Never – don't email but save for later

[Save Search]   [Save and View Results]   [Reset Form]

Set how often you
want to receive emails

View your search results

USAJOBS   Paulina   Help   Search

Keywords   Location
"IT Specialist"   California   Search

You are currently searching on: 1 to 7 of 7 jobs   Sort By:
                                                                                           Relevance ⌄
Keyword: "IT   Remove
Specialist"
                                        IT Specialist   Save Job | More Like This
Location: California Remove
                                        ...This job announcement is for IT Specialist positions for Naval Air Systems...Listed below are some examples of IT Specialist
Grade: 09   Remove   work: Assess policy needs and...abilities to perform the duties of an IT Specialist GS-09. Specialized experience...

Grade: 10   Remove   **Salary:** $48,968.00 - $122,549.00 /   **Department:** Department of the Navy
                                                         Per Year   **Agency:**   Naval Air Systems Command
Grade: 11   Remove   **Series &**   GS-2210-09/13   **Position**   Full Time - Permanent
                                        Grade: **Info:**
                                        Location(s): Multiple Locations (11)   **Who May**   United States Citizens
Refine Your Results By: **Open**   11/23/2016 to 2/20/2017   **Apply:**
                                        Period:
Who May Apply: **Announcement** NE72210-13-
◉ Open to the Public   **Number:**   1853535XXXXXXXXE
○ Federal Employees ❓
▸ Department and Agency

Toggle between "Open to the Public" and "Federal
Employees" to see the different openings

Veterans' Preference Applies to U.S. Citizen Announcements, NOT Federal Employee Announcements

U.S. Citizen Announcements

Veterans' Preference will apply to USAJOBS announcements that are open to all U.S. citizens. Your resume could rise to the top of the list with your 5- or 10-point preference.

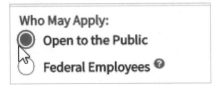

Who May Apply:
- ◉ Open to the Public
- ○ Federal Employees ❓

MANAGEMENT/PROGRAM ANALYST

SECRETARY OF THE NAVY/ASSISTANT FOR ADMINISTRATION (DON/AA)

Agency Contact Information

Few vacancies in the following locations:

📍 Tucson, AZ

Salary Range
$59,246.00 to $160,300.00 / Per Year

Who May Apply
United States Citizens

Federal Employee Announcements

Veterans' Preference will NOT apply to the federal employee announcements. For these announcements, your application alone will compete to get Best Qualified.

Management and Program Analyst

DEFENSE LOGISTICS AGENCY

Agency Contact Information

1 vacancy in the following location:

📍 Battle Creek, MI

Work Schedule is Full Time - Multiple Appointment Types

Opened Friday 1/13/2017
(5 day(s) ago)

Salary Range
$49,765.00 to $64,697.00 / Per Year

Series & Grade
GS-0343-09/09

Supervisory Status
No

Who May Apply
Current Permanent Civilian DLA Employees. ICTAP (Must be in Commuting Area). Individuals eligible for the following Special Appointing Authorities are not required to be in commuting area: Individuals w/Disabilities, Veterans w/a disability rating of 30% or more, Veterans Employment Opportunities Act (VEOA),

---

KEYWORDS FOR RESUME SUCCESS

Find the keywords in the announcement (in bold below) and use them in your resume to demonstrate your qualifications for this job.

Community Recreation Officer, NF-05

ARMY INSTALLATION MANAGEMENT COMMAND

📍 1 vacancy - Wiesbaden, Germany

Work Schedule is Full Time - Permanent

Opened Monday 4/13/2015
(350 day(s) ago)

🕐 Closed Monday 4/27/2015
(336 day(s) ago)

Salary Range
$85,000 to $105,000 / Per Year

Series & Grade
NF-0301-05/05

Promotion Potential
05

Supervisory Status
Yes

Who May Apply
US Citizens and Non-Citizens of a North Atlantic Treaty Organization (NATO) country (except Germany) eligible for employment under U.S. conditions in Germany

Control Number
400706500

Job Announcement Number
EUNAFJD151368909

Keywords in bold

DUTIES:

Through subordinate activity managers, is responsible for overall **management of fiscal resources** and direction of the Directorate, Morale Welfare and Recreation (DMWR) **Community Recreation** Division at a large garrison, to include most of the following programs: **Sports, Fitness and Aquatics**, Extramural Sports Region Championships, Auto Skills, Parks and Picnic Areas, Library, Entertainment, Music and Theater, Arts and Crafts, Community Activity Centers, Outdoor Recreation, Leisure Travel, Better Opportunities for Single Soldiers (BOSS), and non-facility based programs. **Provides leadership and supervision**, and communicates mission and organization goals to subordinates.

Provides policies and guidance to ensure attainment of the established objectives of the division. Directs, develops, and **administers plans and procedures; implements regulations** to provide for a comprehensive community recreation program widely recognized for addressing a **broad range of interests and needs** of the military community. **Institutes innovative programs** to meet future needs, including development and support of **contingency operations** for mobilization and demobilization. **Coordinates and markets program** within the community. **Develops policy and strategic plans** addressing resources, facilities, and programs.

Reviews program priorities and develops five-year plan covering projected programs of personnel, funds, and facilities. Serves as the **Garrison representative and advisor** on matters relating to recreation and morale support of soldiers and their Families.

SPECIALIZED EXPERIENCE IS YOUR POT OF GOLD

The requirements for specialized experience MUST be covered in your federal resume in order to pass the first hurdle and be rated qualified for the position. This is a deal breaker! The HR specialist will be looking for the "One Year Specialized Experience" at the "next lower grade / salary level" in your resume. Learn how to match your resume to the POT of GOLD in the announcement.

QUALIFICATIONS REQUIRED:

Work experience directing/managing one or more DMWR Recreation Programs for a garrison, or similar civilian operation, for at least one year.

Specialized
Experience

Conditions of employment:
1. A one-year probationary period may be required.
2. Meet all qualification/eligibility requirements.
3. Satisfactorily complete an employment verification check.
4. Successfully complete all required background checks.
5. A completed and signed copy DA Form 3433-1 is required prior to entrance on duty.
6. Incumbent is required to submit a Financial Disclosure Statement, OGE-450, Executive Branch Personnel Confidential Financial Disclosure Report upon entering the position and annually, in accordance with DoD Directive 5500-7-R, Joint Ethics Regulation, dated 30 August 1993.
7. Incumbent must file a Confidential Statement of Affiliations and Financial Interest in accordance with the requirements of AR 600-50.

HOW YOU WILL BE EVALUATED:

Applicants who posses the following will be considered as best qualified

1. Experience with RECTRAC or other **automated inventory systems**.
2. Experience with **budgeting and internal controls**?
3. Experience **briefing** senior leadership or civilian equivalent?
4. Experience with **planning and executing large scale events**?
5. Experience with **Installation Status Reports (ISR)** or civilian programs that evaluates facilities infrastructure according to prescribed standards to determine its readiness to meet current and future missions?
6. Experience with Common Levels of Support (CLS) or a civilian equivalent matrix system that **measures operational performance**, effectiveness, and customer satisfaction?

Keywords
in bold

Applicants meeting both minimum qualifications and best qualified criteria will be referred to the selection manager prior to those who meet only the minimum qualifications.

INTELLIGENCE SPECIALIST

NAVAL AIR SYSTEMS COMMAND

📍 1 vacancy - Patuxent River, MD

Work Schedule is Full Time - Excepted Service Permanent

Opened Friday 8/14/2015
(227 day(s) ago)

🕐 Closed Thursday 8/20/2015
(221 day(s) ago)

Salary Range

$43,057 to $55,970 / Per Year

Series & Grade

GG-0132-07/07

Promotion Potential

13

Supervisory Status

No

Keywords in bold

DUTIES:

- Employee performs **basic research and analysis** utilizing **all-source intelligence, databases, assessments, and/or products in support of assigned programs** within the Naval Aviation Enterprise, with a primary focus on intelligence support for Mission, Engineering, and Analysis; PEO Unmanned Aerial Vehicles and Cyber Threats.

- Participate in the **research, formulation, and presentation of oral briefings** and **written products for assigned customers** under the guidance of a senior analyst.

- The analyst will utilize **JWICS, to conduct research, communicate** with other analysts and subject matter experts, and utilize external **intelligence databases**.

QUALIFICATIONS REQUIRED:

In order to qualify for this position, your resume must provide sufficient experience and/or education, knowledge, skills, and abilities, to perform the duties of the specific position. Your resume is the key means we have for evaluating your skills, knowledge, and abilities, as they relate to this position. Therefore, we encourage you to be clear and specific when describing your experience.

Specialized Experience

Your resume must demonstrate at least one year of specialized experience at or equivalent to the GG/GS-07 grade level or pay band in the Federal service equivalent experience in the private or public sector. Specialized experience is defined as experience that is typically in or related to the work of the position to be filled and has equipped you with the particular knowledge, skills, and abilities to successfully perform the duties of the position. Specialized experience must demonstrate the following: **1) Research specific intelligence information in preparation of studies; 2) Extract all significant data pertaining to cyber-based intrusions; 3) Assist senior analysts with providing intelligence products.**

HOW YOU WILL BE EVALUATED:

When the application process is complete, we will review your resume to ensure you meet the hiring eligibility and qualification requirements listed in this announcement. You will be rated based on the information provided in your resume and responses to the questionnaire, along with your supporting documentation to determine your ability to demonstrate the following knowledge, skills and abilities/competencies:
- **RESEARCH**
- **INTELLIGENCE ANALYSIS**
- **INTELLIGENCE DATABASES**

Give yourself all the credit that you can when answering. There are multiple ways to give an E answer. Make sure your answers are supported in your resume!

Questionnaire: Intelligence Specialist

For your information, below is an example of the rating scale that applicants will use to answer competency based assessment questions.

A- I do not have experience or demonstrated capability in performing this activity, but I am willing to learn.

B- I have limited experience in performing this activity. I have had exposure to this activity but would require additional guidance, instruction, or experience to perform it at a satisfactory level.

C- I have a fair amount of experience and a fair amount of demonstrated capability in performing this activity. I can perform this activity satisfactorily but could benefit from additional guidance, instruction, or experience to perform this activity more effectively.

D- I have considerable experience and capability in performing this task. I can perform task independently and effectively.

E- I have extensive experience in performing this task. I am considered an expert; I am able to train or assist others; and my work is typically not reviewed by a supervisor. I have received verbal and/or written recognition from other in carrying out this task.

2. Perform basic **research and analysis** utilizing all source intelligence.

3. Research and assist in the preparation of **briefings and written products** for assigned customers.

4. **Conduct research; communicate** with other analysts and subject matter experts utilizing external **intelligence databases**.

5. Utilize **intelligence regulations and directives** to include intelligence oversight as well as applicable security procedures and policies of collateral and sensitive compartmental information.

6. Participate with higher grade analysts in **researching for specific intelligence information** in preparation of routine **studies** or portions of complex studies.

As previously explained, your responses in this Assessment Questionnaire are subject to evaluation and verification. Later steps in the selection process are specifically designed to verify your responses. Deliberate attempts to falsify information will be grounds for disqualifying you or for dismissing you from employment following acceptance. Please take this opportunity to review your responses to ensure their accuracy.

Keywords in bold

STEP

4

Analyze Vacancy Announcements for Keywords

Keywords are critical for your federal resume!

Photo: Military Spouses attending **The Stars Are Lined Up for Military Spouses** *with Program S presentation by Kathryn Troutman at Army Community Services, Schofield Barracks, Oahu, HI, October 2016*

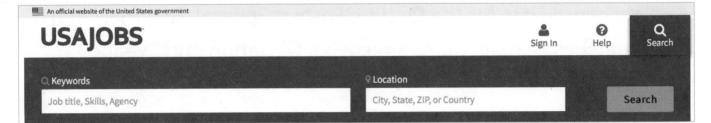

USAJOBS

Sign In   Help   Search

🔍 Keywords

Job title, Skills, Agency

📍 Location

City, State, ZIP, or Country

Search

Steps to Finding Keywords in a Vacancy Announcement

1. Find ONE GOOD target vacancy announcement.

2. You will be reviewing these sections from the announcement for keywords:

   ✪ Duties

   ✪ Qualifications

   ✪ Specialized Experience

   ✪ Questionnaire

   ✪ Agency or organization mission

3. Copy and paste these sections from the announcement into a word processing program such as MS Word.

4. Enlarge the type to 14 or 16 points to make the print more readable.

5. Separate each sentence by increasing the line spacing for the entire document.

6. Delete useless words such as "the incumbent will" or "duties will encompass a variety of tasks including."

7. Underline or highlight keywords and skills that are significant to the position, such as "identifying deficiencies in human performance" and "recommending changes for correction."

How Many Keywords Do I Need?

At a minimum, include at least five to seven keywords and keyword phrases in your resume. However, the more keywords you can include to help translate your experience into terms that the human resources specialist can clearly identify, the greater your chances of having the HR specialist understand how your qualifications match the desired qualifications in the vacancy announcement.

Now MATCH Your Resume to the Keywords

Once you have drafted a basic resume, you MUST MATCH this resume to these keywords. Don't try to use the same resume to apply for a number of different vacancy announcements. The ALL CAP WORDS in an Outline Format resume are phrases and keywords from the announcements. (See more on this in Step 6.) The human resources specialist and supervisor will recognize these skills from their announcement.

Keyword Lists for the Outline Format Federal Resume: Logistics Management Specialist, (Aviation and Weapons Systems) GS 9/13:

Logistics Management Specialist

SECRETARY OF THE NAVY/ASSISTANT FOR ADMINISTRATION (DON/AA)

Agency Contact Information

1 vacancy in the following locations:

♀ China Lake, CA
♀ Point Mugu, CA
♀ San Diego, CA
♀ Jacksonville, FL
♀ Orlando Naval Warfare Center, FL
More Locations (9)

Work Schedule is Full Time - Permanent

Opened Wednesday 11/23/2016
(7 day(s) ago)

🕘 Closes Monday 2/20/2017
(82 day(s) away)

Salary Range
$48,968.00 to $122,549.00 / Per Year

Series & Grade
GS-0346-09/13

Supervisory Status
No

Who May Apply
United States Citizens

Control Number
456864300

Job Announcement Number
NE70346-13-1853339XXXXXXXXE

Based on the various locations of this announcement, vacancies can be filled as GS-09/11/12/13 or DS-03/04/05 pay band (equivalent to GS -09/10, GS-11/12, GS12/13). Promotion is neither implied nor guaranteed.

This is a public notice announcement; under this recruitment procedure, each location/installation, identified in this public notice will make selections for vacancies as they occur. **There may or may not be actual/projected vacancies at the time you submit your application.** Please read this Public Notice in its entirety prior to submitting your application for consideration.

Under this recruitment procedure, each location/installation, identified in this Public Notice will make selections for vacancies as they occur. **There may or may not be actual/projected vacancies at the time you submit your application.**

For the GS11 Specialized experience would include: 1) developing and providing logistics planning data to senior logistics personnel and other support team personnel supporting various aviation systems programs; 2) assisting in the development of an Integrated Logistics Support Plans for assigned programs, defining requirements and providing input to other applicable planning documents. OR 3 full academic years of progressively higher level graduate education or PhD or equivalent graduate degree or LL.M., if in a related field.

To get Best Qualified for this position at the GS-11 level, use these keywords in your Outline Format federal resume:

- DEVELOP AND PROVIDE LOGISTICS PLANNING DATA
- SUPPORT SENIOR LOGISTICS PERSONNEL AND TEAM PERSONNEL
- AVIATION SYSTEMS AND PROGRAMS
- ASSIST IN DEVELOPMENT OF INTEGRATED LOGISTICS SUPPORT PLANS
- DEFINE REQUIREMENTS AND PROVIDE INPUT INTO PLANNING DOCUMENTS

For the GS12 Specialized experience would include: 1) Applying policies, executing processes, following procedures and produce documentation to create an integrated Aviation Logistics and Industrial support package. 2) Providing advice to ensure compliance with environmental regulations associated with supportability and logistics in the acquisition of aircraft, aircraft systems, and weapon systems. 3) Providing continued fleet maintenance and supply support throughout the life cycle of aviation weapon systems or related equipment. 4) Assisting in supportability analyses to solve varied design and logistics issues and make recommendations to ensure the readiness of aircraft/systems are operational and supportability requirements are achieved and affordable.

To get Best Qualified for this position at the GS-12 level, use these keywords in your Outline Format federal resume:

- APPLY POLICIES, EXECUTE PROCESSES AND PROCEDURES TO CREATE INTEGRATED AVIATION LOGISTICS AND INDUSTRIAL SUPPORT PACKAGE
- PROVIDE ADVICE TO ENSURE COMPLIANCE WITH ENVIRONMENTAL REGULATIONS
- SUPPORT AND LOGISTICAL SUPPORT FOR ACQUISTION OF AIRCRAFT AND WEAPON SYSTEMS
- FLEET MAINTENANCE AND SUPPLY SUPPORT
- LIFE CYCLE OF AVIATION WEAPON SYSTEMS
- SUPPORTABILITY ANALYSIS TO SOLVE VARIED DESIGN AND LOGISTICS ISSUES
- MAKE RECOMMENDATIONS TO ENSURE READINESS OF AIRCRAFT/SYSTEMS

The Occupational Assessment Questionnaire for this position can provide additional keywords and phrases:

A- I have no experience performing this task.

B- I have limited experience in performing this work behavior. I have had exposure to this work behavior but would require additional guidance, instruction, or experience to perform it at a proficient level.

C- I have experience performing this work behavior across routine or predictable situations with minimal supervision or guidance.

D- I have performed this work behavior independently across a wide range of situations. I have assisted others in carrying out this work behavior. I seek guidance in carry out this work behavior only in unusually complex situations.

E- I am considered an expert in carrying out this work behavior. I advise and instruct others in carrying out this work behavior on a regular basis. I am consulted by my colleagues and/or superiors to carry out this work behavior in unusually complex situations.

7. Ensure maintainability, readiness, supportability, and affordability through a series of Supportability Analysis for the Maintenance Planning Process.

8. Utilizing design interface and maintenance planning tools and procedures to plan, establish, and execute effective total life cycle support.

9. Facilitate the application of logistics concepts and policies across the program, in support of program goals for the Department.

10. Provide logistics expertise to Weapons Systems Program Offices and Logistics Managers to ensure the designed logistics support systems meet established supportability requirements.

11. Establish processes and guidelines that ensure the supportability analyses performed result in successful identification of maintenance requirements and support alternatives.

12. Provide analysis and responses during the development and review of program Contractor Data Requirements Lists and Statements of Work for the Department.

More keywords and phrases from the Questionnaire:

- SUPPORTABILITY ANALYSIS FOR MAINTENANCE PLANNING PROCESS
- UTILIZE DESIGN INTERFACE AND MAINTENANCE PLANNING TOOLS
- FACILITATE APPLICATION OF LOGISTICS CONCEPTS
- PROVIDE LOGISTICS EXPERTISE TO WEAPONS SYSTEMS PROGRAM OFFICES
- ESTABLISH PROCESSES AND GUIDELINES FOR SUPPORABILITY ANALYSIS

Administrative Management Specialist, GS-0301-09/12

This announcement is open to all Current, Permanent, Competitive Service OPM Employees, and Land Management Eligibles.

Administrative Management Specialist

OFFICE OF PERSONNEL MANAGEMENT

Agency Contact Information

1 vacancy in the following location:

📍 Washington DC, DC

Work Schedule is Full Time - Agency Employees Only

Opened Tuesday 11/22/2016
(8 day(s) ago)

🕒 Closes Wednesday 12/7/2016
(7 day(s) away)

Salary Range
$53,435.00 to $100,736.00 / Per Year

Series & Grade
GS-0301-09/12

Promotion Potential
12

Supervisory Status
No

Who May Apply
Current, Permanent, Competitive Service OPM Employees, and Land Management Eligibles

Control Number
457060400

Job Announcement Number
17-063-RGJ-OPM

Job Overview

Summary

This position is located in the Office of the Executive Secretariat, where the selectee will serve as an Executive Assistant within the Office of the Director.

Duties

- Oversee management of all communications - regular and electronic mail, telephone calls, and personal visits.

- Collaborate with Associate Directors/Office Heads and other senior staff to ensure that the supervisor is briefed appropriately.

- Act as a key liaison with OPM's Associate Directors and senior staff.

- Review and analyze incoming and outgoing correspondence, determining clarity, appropriateness and accuracy of information provided, as well as ensuring the view of the supervisor is clearly depicted.

- Create travel itineraries, making all arrangements, including agenda items and arranging visits with committed parties.

For the GS-11 Grade Level: Applicants must have one year of specialized experience at the GS-09 level serving as administrative specialist, performing the following duties: scheduling office travel for multiple staff members including executive senior staff, overseeing management of all official communication, advising staff on sensitive issues, and acting as key liaison with senior executive leadership.

OR Possess a Ph.D. or equivalent doctoral degree, or three years of progressively higher graduate education leading to such a degree. Education demonstrates the knowledge, skills, and abilities necessary to do the work of this position.

OR An equivalent combination of specialized experience and graduate level education.

For the GS-12 Grade Level: Applicants must have one year of specialized experience at the GS-11 level serving as administrative specialist, performing the following duties: scheduling office travel for multiple staff members including executive senior staff and associate director, overseeing management of all official communication, advising executive staff on sensitive issues, acting as key liaison with senior executive leadership, arranging conferences (ensuring calendars are properly cleared and committed, materials are prepared and distributed to participants etc).

To get Best Qualified for this position at the GS-11 or 12 level, use these keywords in your Outline Format federal resume:

GS-11 Keywords

- ADMINISTRATIVE SPECIALIST
- SCHEDULE OFFICE TRAVEL
- OVERSEE MANAGEMENT OF OFFICIAL COMMUNICATION
- STAFF ADVISOR
- KEY LIAISON WITH SENIOR LEADERSHIP
- ORAL AND WRITTEN COMMUNICATION

GS-12 Keywords

- ADMINISTRATIVE SPECIALIST
- SCHEDULE OFFICE TRAVEL
- OVERSEE MANAGEMENT OF OFFICIAL COMMUNICATION
- STAFF ADVISOR
- KEY LIAISON WITH SENIOR LEADERSHIP
- ORAL AND WRITTEN COMMUNICATION
- PLAN AND ARRANGE CONFERENCES

The Questionnaire will be written based upon these skills and competencies:

How You Will Be Evaluated

We will review your application package to ensure you meet the job and eligibility requirements. Your application packag
verified, your rating will be changed to an appropriate level, based on your application package.

All applicants will be rated on the following Skills or Competencies:

- **Oral Communication**
- **Written Communication**
- **Administrative Experience**

The best qualified applicants will be referred to the hiring manager for consideration.

The Occupational Assessment Questionnaire for this position can provide additional keywords and phrases:

A- I have not had education, training or experience in performing this task.
B- I have had education or training in performing the task, but have not yet performed it on the job.
C- I have performed this task on the job. My work on this task was monitored closely by a supervisor or senior employee to ensure complia
D- I have performed this task as a regular part of a job. I have performed it independently and normally without review by a supervisor or s
E- I am considered an expert in performing this task. I have supervised performance of this task or am normally the person who is consulte
them in doing this task because of my expertise.

4. Oversee management of regular and electronic mail, telephone calls, and personal visits to the supervisor.

5. Collaborate with Associate Directors and other senior executives to ensure that the supervisor is briefed appropriately.

6. Act as a key liaison with senior executives and senior staff.

7. Prepare or coordinate recurring and other reports, and respond to senior management requests on routine actions/requests.

8. Review proposals, inquiries, recommendations and other communications forwarded to the supervisor.

9. Determine what receives the supervisor's attention and assures that appropriate background information is provided.

10. Review and analyze incoming and outgoing correspondence, determining clarity, appropriateness and accuracy of information provided,
the supervisor is clearly depicted.

Additional keywords for your resume:

- OVERSEE COMMUNICATIONS AND BRIEFINGS WITH THE SUPERVISOR
- PREPARE AND COORDINATE REPORTS
- REVIEW PROPOSALS AND RECOMMENDATIONS FORWARDED TO THE SUPERVISOR
- ANALYZE AND REVIEW CORRESPONDENCE

Management and Program Analyst, GS-0304-09/12
Current Federal Employees + VEOA, VRA, and Others

MANAGEMENT AND PROGRAM ANALYST

CITIZENSHIP AND IMMIGRATION SERVICES

Agency Contact Information

8 vacancies in the following locations:

📍 Washington DC, DC
📍 Bloomington, MN

Work Schedule is Full Time - Permanent

Opened Tuesday 11/29/2016
(1 day(s) ago)

🕐 Closes Thursday 12/8/2016
(8 day(s) away)

Salary Range
$42,823.00 to $80,731.00 / Per Year

Series & Grade
GS-0343-09/12

Promotion Potential
12

Supervisory Status
No

Who May Apply
Current or Former Federal Employees with Competitive Status; Reinstatement Eligibles; OPM Interchange Agreement Eligibles; VEOA, VRA (Up to GS-11 Only), Disability, Surplus/Displaced Eligibles.

Control Number
457302400

Job Announcement Number
CIS-1856748-IDP

Qualifications required:

GS-11: In addition to the requirements at the lower grade level(s), you qualify at the GS-11 level if you possess one (1) year of specialized experience, equivalent to at least the GS-09 level in the federal government, which has equipped you with the skills needed to successfully perform the duties of the position. You must have experience performing the following duties:

- Conducting studies to identify, analyze, and recommend solutions to problems in program operations.

- Using analytical techniques and statistics to assess issues related to management processes, systems and support programs. **OR**

- You may also substitute successful completion of a Ph.D. or equivalent doctoral degree, or 3 full years of progressively higher-level graduate education leading to such a degree in an accredited college or university, may be substituted for experience at the GS-11 grade level. Such education must demonstrate the skills needed to do the work. A course of study in business administration, public administration, or related fields is qualifying. One year of full-time graduate education is considered to be the number of credit hours that the school attended has determined to represent 1 year of full-time study. If that information cannot be obtained from the school, 54 semester hours should be considered as satisfying the 3 years of full-time study requirement.

To get Best Qualified for this position at the GS-11 level, use these keywords in your Outline Format federal resume:

- CONDUCT STUDIES
- IDENTIFY, ANALYZE AND RECOMMEND SOLUTIONS TO PROBLEMS
- UTILIZE ANALYTICAL TECHNIQUES AND STATISTICS
- ANALYZE MANAGEMENT PROCESSES, SYSTEMS AND/OR SUPPORT PROGRAMS

GS-12: In addition to the requirements at the lower grade level(s), you qualify at the GS-12 level if you possess one (1) year of specialized experience, equivalent to at least the GS-11 level in the federal government, which has equipped you with the skills needed to successfully perform the duties of the position. You must have experience performing the following duties:

- Conducting studies, analyzing findings and making recommendations on program operations.

- Conducting detailed analyses of complex functions and work processes.

- Participating in special studies.

- Supporting the development and evaluation of policies and recommending actions to achieve program objectives and improvements.

To get Best Qualified for this position at the GS-12 level, add these keywords to the list above in your Outline Format federal resume:

- CONDUCT SPECIAL STUDIES
- DETAILED ANALYSIS OF COMPLEX FUNCTIONS AND WORK PROCESSES
- DEVELOP AND EVALUATE POLICIES AND RECOMMEND ACTIONS

Questionnaire:

For each item, select the ONE response that most accurately describes your current level of experience and capability using the scale below.

A- I have not had education, training or experience in performing this task.
B- I have had education or training in performing this task, but have not yet performed it on the job.
C- I have performed this task on the job. My work on this task was monitored closely by a supervisor or senior employee to ensure compliance with proper procedures.
D- I have performed this task as a regular part of a job. I have performed it independently and normally without review by a supervisor or senior employee.
E- I am considered an expert in performing this task. I have supervised performance of this task or am normally the person who is consulted by other workers to assist them in doing this task because of my expertise.

6. Verifies accuracy of data and reconciles errors or inconsistencies.

7. Analyze or interprets data or other information.

8. Ability to understand, organize, and analyze in order to provide written and oral responses with conclusions, alternatives and recommendations to address issues raised concerning lock box operations.

9. Reviews documents, records or data consistently to verify completeness, correctness, compliance or authenticity.

10. Is open to change and adapts work methods in response to new information, changing conditions or unexpected obstacles.

11. Communicates information- orally and in writing- in a clear, succinct, respectful and organized manner through a variety of media; produces written information that is appropriate for the intended audience.

12. Contacts others-orally and in writing- to obtain and provide information.

Keywords from the Questionnaire: the Questionnaire will be more specific and technical than the duties or the Specialized Experience. You can find more keywords and descriptions to use in the Duties and Responsibilities.

- SPECIAL STUDIES (verify accuracy of data, reconcile errors)
- ANALYZE AND INTERPRET DATA
- PROVIDE WRITTEN AND ORAL RESPONSES TO QUESTIONS AND RECOMMENDATIONS
- RECOMMEND CHANGES (adapt work methods in response to new information, changing conditions)
- ANALYZE MANAGEMENT PROCESSES, SYSTEMS AND/OR SUPPORT PROGRAMS

Your Outline Format federal resume MUST include the following information: (using the USAJOBS resume builder is highly recommended!)

Please read the following important information to ensure we have everything we need to consider your application:

It is your responsibility to ensure your responses and appropriate documentation is submitted prior to the closing date. Your resume serves as the basis for qualification determinations and must highlight your most relevant and significant work experience and education (if applicable), as it relates to **this** job opportunity. Please be clear and specific when describing your work history as we cannot make assumptions regarding your experience. Your application will also be rated and ranked among others based on your responses to the online questions.

Please ensure EACH work history includes ALL of the following information:

- Job Title (include series and grade if Federal Job)
- Duties (be specific in describing your duties)
- Employer's name and address
- Supervisor name and phone number
- Start and end dates including month, day and year (e.g. June 18 2007 to April 05 2008)
- Start and end dates for each grade/pay level if you've held a federal position.
- Full-time or part-time status (include hours worked per week)
- Salary

The Factor Evaluation System (FES) is part of the Classification Standards and includes nine factors that are part of most nonsupervisory GS positions. These descriptions are used for assigning grades under the GS system and are highly useful for improving your resume.

Look through the FES definitions in the Classification Standard for your target position. Where applicable, add the answers to the following key FES questions into your resume to dramatically improve your federal resume content.

KNOWLEDGE

- What knowledge do you have to help you do your job?

SUPERVISORY CONTROLS

- What kind of supervisory control do you have?
- Or do you work independently?

GUIDELINES USED

- What guidelines do you use to do your job?
- What laws, regulations or references?
- List all legislation, manuals, SOPs, policies, references

COMPLEXITY

- How complex are the duties of your position?

SCOPE & EFFECT

- Who do you talk to and work with?
- What is the scope of your work?
- Is it local, regional, worldwide?

PERSONAL CONTACTS AND PURPOSE OF CONTACTS

- Who are your customers?
- Are they nearby or do you work with them through email, etc.?
- How many customers do you support?

Before Resume: WITHOUT THE FES INFORMATION

> **Administrative Assistant (40 hrs per wk) (Massachusetts Air National Guard) Jan 08 – Present.** Provide administrative support to the Chief of Staff (Massachusetts Air National Guard). Provide reports to queries on personnel matters utilizing data systems RCAS and IPERMS. Track suspense's, Executive Summaries, correspondence, briefings, and investigations utilizing an electronic log system. Review Executive Summaries for content, format, and administrative errors. Maintain Payroll Worksheets for 35 personnel monitoring hours worked and vacations taken, and provide summary reports to supervisors and finance personnel. Manage Moral and Welfare fund requests for Massachusetts National Guard units by reviewing requests for legality, administrative correctness, submitting the paperwork to the State Military Department, and coordinating issuance of checks. Monitor the Chief of Staff's calendar for appointments and events. Assist in developing/mentoring new personnel both enlisted and officer with office procedures.

After Resume: WITH THE FES INFORMATION

> **ADMINISTRATIVE ASSISTANT (40 hrs per wk) (Mass. Air National Guard)**
> Assistant to the Chief of Staff who oversees 3,000 Mass. National Guard Soldiers. Work independently to support all administrative, personnel, correspondence and payroll administration for the director.
>
> **COMPLEX ADMINISTRATION:** Highly skilled in supporting multiple battalion deployments and re-integration and readiness during and following the ending of Iraq and Afghanistan. ACCOMPLISHMENT: Improved support for deployed and emergency support for the guardsmen. Organized and coordinated efficient ceremonies and events. Managed paperwork for complex deployments.
>
> **IMPLEMENT THE NATIONAL GUARD TECHNICIAN HANDBOOK.** Implement and administer "The Technician Act of 1968", Public Law 90-486, for all support services for Reserves and Active duty personnel.
>
> **REPORTS AND DATABASE ADMINISTRATION AND COMPUTER SKILLS.** Produce reports to queries on personnel matters utilizing data systems RCAS and IPERMS. Track suspenses, Executive Summaries, correspondence, briefings, and investigations utilizing an electronic log system.
>
> **CUSTOMER SERVICES FOR THE GUARD PERSONNEL:** Manage Morale and Welfare fund requests for Massachusetts National Guard units by reviewing requests for legality and administrative correctness, submitting the paperwork to the State Military Department, and coordinating issuance of checks.

www.onetonline.org/

O*NET OnLine is an excellent source for keywords for federal, private sector, and LinkedIn resumes.

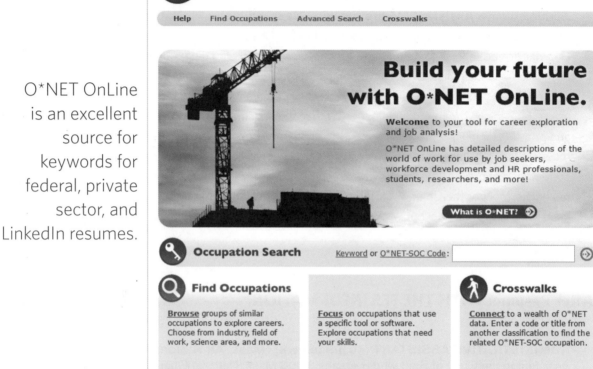

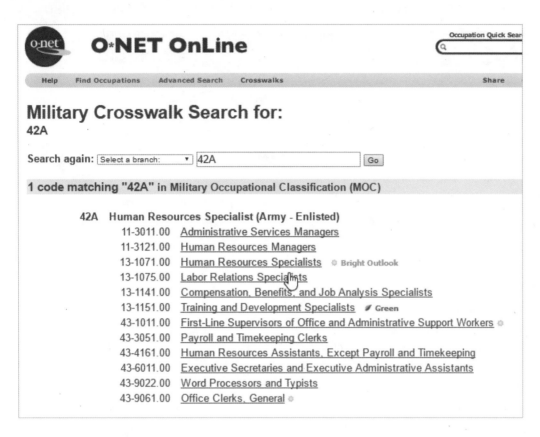

https://acpol2.army.mil/fasclass/search_fs/search_fasclass.asp

If you are looking for a DOD or U.S. Army Civilian position, this Position Description database is invaluable for writing your federal resume.

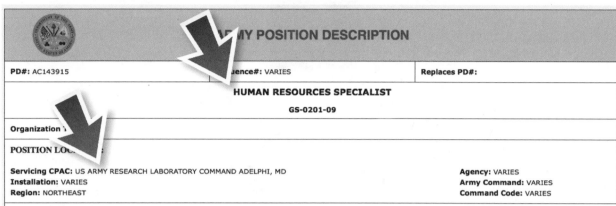

ARMY POSITION DESCRIPTION

PD#: AC143915	...uence#: VARIES	Replaces PD#:

HUMAN RESOURCES SPECIALIST

GS-0201-09

Organization

POSITION LO...

Servicing CPAC: US ARMY RESEARCH LABORATORY COMMAND ADELPHI, MD
Installation: VARIES
Region: NORTHEAST

Agency: VARIES
Army Command: VARIES
Command Code: VARIES

POSITION CLASSIFICATION STANDARDS USED IN CLASSIFYING/GRADING POSITION:

Citation 1: JFS ADMIN WORK IN HR MANAGEMENT GRP, GS-0200, DTD DEC 2000

Supervisory Certification: *I certify that this is an accurate statement of the major duties and responsibilities of this position and its organizational relationships, and that the position is necessary to carry out Government functions for which I am responsible. This certification is made with the knowledge that this information is to be used for statutory purposes relating to appointment and payment of public funds, and that false or misleading statements may constitute violations of such statutes or their*

POSITION DUTIES:

1. Provides technical assistance to supervisor and/or employees in support of a variety of personnel activities to include workers compensation, thrift savings plan program, permanent change of station (PCS), and leave administration.

2. Coordinates Thrift Savings Plan open seasons. Ensures program information for assigned program is disseminated to workforce on a timely basis. Provides assistance and counseling to the workforce on the program. Processes permanent change of station (PCS) requests and entitlements.

3. Administers the Leave Program. Provides advice and guidance to customers on the numerous aspects of the various leave programs. Topics such as Family and Medical Leave, Military leave, voluntary leave transfer program, court leave, as well as sick and annual leave are included. Drafts the local program implementation procedures and guidance for installation. Ensures leave program information is widely publicized.
25%

4. Assembles pre-employment information for employees, provides orientation to new employees. Explains basic rules, regulations, and policies regarding employment at Fort Monmouth, provides assistance and guidance with in-processing requirements. Provides brochures and brief explanations of benefits. Responds to customer inquiries on such matters as procedures for filing applications, status of recruitment, kinds of vacancies, etc. Researches regulations, policies, and guidance to obtain and support answers. Answers customer questions regarding internal/external recruitment and provides them with appropriate forms.
25%

5. Incumbent is responsible for administering the CECOM Office of Workers Compensation Program (OWCP). Administration includes the overall planning and direction and timely execution of the Compensation Program. Serves as an advisor and obtains management's cooperation and support in accepting and implementing the compensation program to include returning injured employees back to work as soon as possible. Conducts analysis that includes such factors as accident rates, adequacy of facilities and services, inconsistencies in reporting data and other factors. Prepares statistical data for quarterly and annual reports that are used by AMC and DA in determining OWCP trends and associated fiscal analysis. Provides narrative that expounds on required reports. Fosters an awareness of the program by publishing articles in various media. Educates the workforce by conducting training, performing briefings and advising managers. Incumbent responds to inquires from all sources: employees, higher headquarters, doctor's offices, and various OWCP offices. Utilizes the Civilian Resource Conservation Program to direct the combined activity resources to develop a safe work environment by reducing the total number of accidents.
50%

Performs other duties as assigned.

KNOWLEDGE REQUIRED BY THE POSITION FACTOR 1-6 950 POINTS

Incumbent must have the knowledge of and skill in applying, fundamental Human Resources Methods, principles and practices. Advises and resolves moderately complex, non-controversial, well-precedent factual, procedural and recurring issues for which there are one or more readily apparent solutions. Make informed judgments on problems and issues. Analyze segments of Human Resources problems or issues related to immediate problems of limited scope.

Keywords for your resume based on the position duties:
technical assistance, support personnel activities, ensure program information, process change of station requests, administer leave program, new employment pre-employment information and orientation, Workers Compensation Program, advisor, conduct training, human resources methods

STEP

5

Analyze Your Core Competencies

Core Competencies can help your federal resume stand out with a hiring manager!

Photo: Husband of a Military Spouse asking questions about PPP-S for his wife. They just PCS'ed to Schofield Barracks, October 2016.

Office of Personnel Management (OPM) Competencies

Find your core competencies and check them off the list. Add a few of these competencies into the "duties" section of your work experience.

Interpersonal Effectiveness

- ❑ Builds and sustains positive relationships.
- ❑ Handles conflicts and negotiations effectively.
- ❑ Builds and sustains trust and respect.
- ❑ Collaborates and works well with others.
- ❑ Shows sensitivity and compassion for others.
- ❑ Encourages shared decision-making.
- ❑ Recognizes and uses ideas of others.
- ❑ Communicates clearly, both orally and in writing.
- ❑ Listens actively to others.
- ❑ Honors commitments and promises.

Customer Service

- ❑ Understands that customer service is essential to achieving our mission.
- ❑ Understands and meets the needs of internal customers.
- ❑ Manages customer complaints and concerns effectively and promptly.
- ❑ Designs work processes and systems that are responsive to customers.
- ❑ Ensures that daily work and the strategic direction are customer-centered.
- ❑ Uses customer feedback data in planning and providing products and services.
- ❑ Encourages and empowers subordinates to meet or exceed customer needs and expectations.
- ❑ Identifies and rewards behaviors that enhance customer satisfaction.

Flexibility/Adaptability

- ❑ Responds appropriately to new or changing situations.
- ❑ Handles multiple inputs and tasks simultaneously.
- ❑ Seeks and welcomes the ideas of others.
- ❑ Works well with all levels and types of people.
- ❑ Accommodates new situations and realities.
- ❑ Remains calm in high-pressure situations.
- ❑ Makes the most of limited resources.
- ❑ Demonstrates resilience in the face of setbacks.
- ❑ Understands change management.

Creative Thinking

- ❑ Appreciates new ideas and approaches.
- ❑ Thinks and acts innovatively.
- ❑ Looks beyond current reality and the "status quo".
- ❑ Demonstrates willingness to take risks.
- ❑ Challenges assumptions.
- ❑ Solves problems creatively.
- ❑ Demonstrates resourcefulness.
- ❑ Fosters creative thinking in others.
- ❑ Allows and encourages employees to take risks.
- ❑ Identifies opportunities for new projects and acts on them.
- ❑ Rewards risk-taking and non-successes and values what was learned.

Systems Thinking

- ❑ Understands the complexities of the agency and how the "product" is delivered.
- ❑ Appreciates the consequences of specific actions on other parts of the system.
- ❑ Thinks in context.
- ❑ Knows how one's role relates to others in the organization.
- ❑ Demonstrates awareness of the purpose, process, procedures, and outcomes of one's work.
- ❑ Encourages and rewards collaboration.

Organizational Stewardship

- ❑ Demonstrates commitment to people.
- ❑ Empowers and trusts others.
- ❑ Develops leadership skills and opportunities throughout organization.
- ❑ Develops team-based improvement processes.
- ❑ Promotes future-oriented system change.
- ❑ Supports and encourages lifelong learning throughout the organization.
- ❑ Manages physical, fiscal, and human resources to increase the value of products and services.
- ❑ Builds links between individuals and groups in the organization.
- ❑ Integrates organization into the community.
- ❑ Accepts accountability for self, others, and the organization's development.
- ❑ Works to accomplish the organizational business plan.

Many federal agencies are creating their own list of core competencies and technical skills required for their positions. These DHS competencies and technical skills would e critical for a Best Qualified federal resume.

From the Security Specialist Competencies: An Interagency Security Committee Guidelines
https://www.dhs.gov/publication/isc-security-specialist-competencies-guideline

Security and National/Federal Policies and Standards
- Interagency Security Committee
- Facility Security Committees
- ISC Facility Security Level Determination Standard
- ISC Risk Management Process
- ISC's Physical Security Criteria for Federal Facilities Standard and Design-Basis Threat Report
- Crime Prevention Through Environmental Design (CPTED)
- National Infrastructure Protection Plan (NIPP)
- National Fire Protection Association
- All Agency Specific Policies/Standards

Facility Security Assessments
- Types of Security Assessments
- Components of a Security Assessment

Information Security
Security of Federal Automated Information Resources
Personnel Security
Operations Security
Industrial Security
Personal Identifiable Information
Communications Security
Continuity of Operations
Occupant Emergency Plan
Incident Management

Personal Identity Verification (PIV) Card Systems
- Personal Identity Verification Card
- Physical Access Control Systems

Basic Physical Security Countermeasures
- Intrusion Detection Systems
- Access Control Systems
- Video Monitoring Systems
- Biometrics
- Protective Lighting
- Security Barriers
- Storage/Safes
- Security Locks and Locking Devices
- Crime Prevention and Security Awareness
- Security Force Specification and Management
- Inspections

Communication Skills
- Report Writing
- Verbal/Speech
- Problem Solving/Decision-making

Contracting Administration
- Contracting Officer's Technical Representative (COTR)

Administrative Skills
Health and Safety

ENTRY LEVEL

Description: These competencies identify the Knowledge, Skills and Abilities required to perform basic safety and occupational health management functions. Duties are performed under the direct supervision or technical leadership of a senior safety professional. Emphasis at the entry level is on developing and acquiring work skills with movement to developmental level.

I. Bureau Orientation and Administration

    A. Government and bureau organization and function
    B. Bureau philosophy and mission
    C. Diversity
    D. Workers' Compensation (OWCP)

II. Standards, Regulations and Procedures

    A. Safety, health and fire codes
    B. Hazard recognition
    C. Inspection and survey techniques
    D. Accident investigation
    E. Accident recording and reporting
    F. NPS-50 and 485 DM
    G. Basic industrial hygiene techniques
    H. Ergonomics
    I. Personal Protective Equipment
    J. Visitor safety

III. Safety Management

    A. Safety/Risk Management
    B. Regulatory compliance; laws and regulations
    C. Safety and Occupational Health program management

IV. Communication

    A. Interpersonal communication skills
    B. Writing basic reports and instructions
    C. Computer skills; DOS, Windows, word processing, Dbase
    D. Basic instructional skills

V. Training and Development

    A. Preparation of instructional materials
    B. Informal field workplace instruction

VI. Supervisory and Management - None

Knowledge, Skills and Abilities

- Knowledge of bureau mission, policy and guidelines.

- Knowledge of safety and health standards and regulations.

- Basic knowledge of procedures and application of safety and health standards.

- Basic knowledge of safety management and legal compliance.

- Ability to provide instruction to small groups.

Source: https://www.nps.gov/training/npsonly/RSK/safeocc.htm

Office of Personnel Management, Senior Executive Service (SES) Executive Core Qualifications (ECQs)

Leading Change	Leading People	Results Driven	Business Acumen	Building Coalitions
Definitions				
This core qualification involves the ability to bring about strategic change, both within and outside the organization, to meet organizational goals. Inherent to this ECQ is the ability to establish an organizational vision and to implement it in a continuously changing environment.	This core qualification involves the ability to lead people toward meeting the organization's vision, mission, and goals. Inherent to this ECQ is the ability to provide an inclusive workplace that fosters the development of others, facilitates cooperation and teamwork, and supports constructive resolution of conflicts.	This core qualification involves the ability to meet organizational goals and customer expectations. Inherent to this ECQ is the ability to make decisions that produce high-quality results by applying technical knowledge, analyzing problems, and calculating risks.	This core qualification involves the ability to manage human, financial, and information resources strategically.	This core qualification involves the ability to build coalitions internally and with other federal agencies, state and local governments, nonprofit and private sector organizations, foreign governments, or international organizations to achieve common goals.
Competencies				
Creativity and Innovation External Awareness Flexibility Resilience Strategic Thinking Vision	Conflict Management Leveraging Diversity Developing Others Team Building	Accountability Customer Service Decisiveness Entrepreneurship Problem Solving Technical Credibility	Financial Management Human Capital Management Technology Management	Partnering Political Savvy Influencing/ Negotiating

More information and samples: *The New SES Application 2nd Edition* by Kathryn Troutman and Diane Hudson

STEP

Write Your Outline Format and Paper Federal Resumes

The **OUTLINE FORMAT FEDERAL RESUME** is the **BEST** format for the USAJOBS Resume Builder. Veterans can use VRA to market their resumes and qualifications directly to hiring managers in a non-competitive application.

Photo: Josephine T. Barrientos, Division Administrative Officer, Civilian Personnel Advisory Liaison, HQ, 25th Infantry Div., Oahu, Hawaii

The federal resume is a reverse chronological resume.

Transition GPS and Private Industry Resume	Federal Resume
Typically 1-2 pages	**3-5 pages based on specific character lengths (use full character lengths if possible)**
Creative use of bold, underline, and other graphics	Reverse chronological resume; traditional format with no graphics, use CAPS for the USAJOBS Builder Resume
No federal elements required (i.e., SSN, supervisor's name and phone, salary, veterans' preference, etc.)	Required: compliance details for each position for the last 10 years (i.e. month and years; street address, zip code, city, state, zip, country; supervisor's name; salary / GS level / military rank)
Short accomplishment bullets focused on results	Accomplishment stories are critical, so your resume will stand out and help you get Best Qualified
Branded "headline"	KSAs must be covered in the resume to demonstrate your specialized experience
Keywords are important	Keywords are imperative
Focus on accomplishments; less detail for position descriptions	Use blend of accomplishments and duties description with details
Profit motivated, product oriented, select customer base	Fiscal responsibility and grants, budgets, cost control, implementation of programs, legislation, serving the American public

Additional Special Considerations for Military

Military	Federal Resume
List dates of Reserve service and active duty service	**Include approx. average hours for Reserve service**, i.e., 20 years of Reserve service with deployments, equals six years of full-time work at 52 weeks per year
Include applicable awards and indicate justification for attaining award	List most awards and honors and include justification
Translate military acronyms and jargon	Translate most military acronyms and jargon, but use acronyms if the vacancy announcement uses the acronyms (i.e., DOD, DON, USMC, etc.)
Quantify and qualify military activities or acronyms	Quantify and qualify military activities or acronyms
Only include military schools/education related to the announcement	Include military service schools; indicate resident classes and total hours

Federal Resume Format

Use the "Outline Format" federal resume style. Since USAJOBS is a resume / application system where HR specialists (NOT an automated system) will read each resume, it is VERY important that the resume be easy to read. The recommended format throughout this book is the Outline Format, which is preferred by HR specialists. The ALL CAP KEYWORDS (or Hats You Wear at Work) are taken from the announcement. They are simple, direct, and match the job announcement and your top-level skills that relate to the target position.

Don't use the bullet format for your resume. Is your resume a laundry list of bullets that are unrelated and not targeted to a job announcement or job series? This format will not help the Human Resources specialists to determine your qualifications for the vacancy announcement.

Avoid the old-school big block format. This format was popular for the Resumix keyword scanning system that was eliminated in 2010. Now, actual humans look at your resume, and large blocks of text are difficult to read.

You MUST include the compliance information required by the Office of Personnel Management (OPM): Month and year and hours per week; employer's street address, city, state, zip code; supervisor phone number; yes/no on whether supervisor may be contacted.

Use the USAJOBS builder. We recommend that you copy and paste your Outline Format resume into the builder, so that all of the information is complete for the HR reviewer.

Work Experience

Make sure that you're actually qualified for the job. Read your target job announcement from beginning to end. Contact the hiring manager listed in the announcement if you're not sure.

Match your work experience section to the target position by using keywords from the announcement. You must use the language from the target job announcement to write your duties, responsibilities, and accomplishments.

Include your best accomplishments in the work experience section. Hiring officials want to read about your unique contributions to your job. Demonstrate that you are a star performer and not just an average one.

Include your Guard or Reserves experience and deployment details.

Education and Training

Education should be in reverse chronological order. Your current or most recent education should be at the beginning of your job block.

Expand your education section beyond just the degree and the college name. Add a list of courses and/or descriptions of three significant projects.

For training, include classroom hours and the certification title. Remove trainings that you took more than 10 years ago.

More samples and details: *Student's Federal Career Guide, 3rd Ed.*, K. Troutman and P. Binkley.

A federal resume should be three to five pages in length.
A one- to two-page resume does not have enough details
about your experience to determine your qualifications.
Resumes longer than five pages give too much information for
the HR specialist to find your skills and abilities.

Writing Style

A profile or "summary of skills" does NOT increase your application score. Your work experience must be anchored to dates, and all verbiage should be tailored to your target job. Do not include a list of generic skills.

Use active, not passive, voice. Avoid phrases such as: responsible for, duties include, assisted with, performed, provide, helped with, tasked with, recruited for, participated in, in addition to, etc. Passive verbs create wordiness and show hiring officials that you are merely a helper at work.

Take out as many acronyms and technical jargon as possible and replace with plain English. Make sure that anyone outside of your line of work can understand your resume, even if the hiring officials are in your field.

Use "I" very minimally in your resume.

Federal HR only wants to see recent and relevant experience. Remove job blocks older than 20 years (for higher grade employees) and 10 years (for lower grade employees).

How to Start Writing

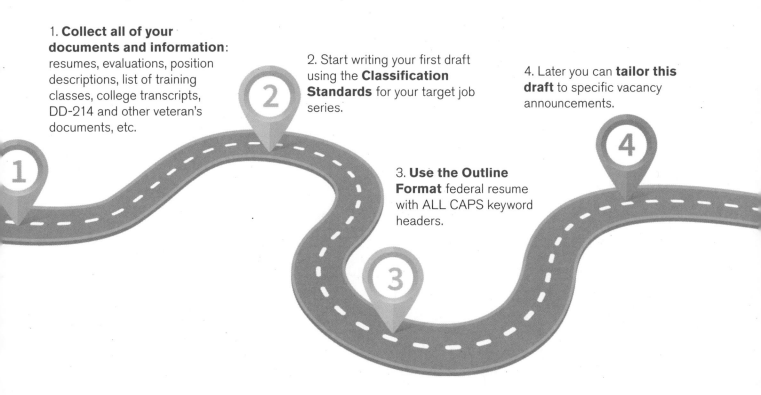

1. **Collect all of your documents and information**: resumes, evaluations, position descriptions, list of training classes, college transcripts, DD-214 and other veteran's documents, etc.

2. Start writing your first draft using the **Classification Standards** for your target job series.

3. **Use the Outline Format** federal resume with ALL CAPS keyword headers.

4. Later you can **tailor this draft** to specific vacancy announcements.

Logistics and Supply

BEFORE: Block Style

HSC/640ᵗʰ ASB (AD) (Operation Enduring Freedom (Spartan Shield)

Camp Udairi, Kuwait (Currently Deployed)
201510–Present / Return Date: TBD/Approx: AUG 2016
Logistics/SASMO Information System Operator, 92A30/25U30 (E6)
Support the Commanders vision and policies under (AR 710-2). Monitors the success of 640ᵗʰ
ASB Bravo Company by overseeing the successful implementation of the (Unit Level Logistics
System-Aviation) ULLS-AE program in conjunction with their operations in the theater of
operations. Supports in the ordering in (ULLS-A (E) and Standard **Army** Maintenance System-
Enhanced (**SAMS-E**) systems over 5 million dollar monthly in maintenance parts expenditures.
Support actions to troubleshoot and resolve program issues experienced by Logistic Information
Systems (LIS) users within the 40th CAB and units operating in 40th CAB area of operations.
Provides technical assistance, resolves problems for information services support personnel,
functional users and functional staff. Provide desktop computer support which includes
diagnosing and resolving any workstation operating system software for (ULLS-A (E), SAMS-E
and (PBUSE**)** Property Book Unit Supply Enhanced application software or hardware problems.

AFTER: Easier to Read

Logistics/SASMO Information System Operator
HSC/640th ASB (AD)
Operation Enduring Freedom - Spartan Shield
Camp Udairi, Kuwait E6
Sustainment Automation Support Management Office (SASMO)

Oct 2015–Present
40 hours / week

SUPPLY AND LOGISTICS SYSTEM IMPLEMENTATION
Expert logistics guidance and oversight, including critical support for the Commander's vision and Army supply policies. Monitor and ensure the success of critical supply and infrastructure support for 640th ASB Bravo Company. Oversee successful implementation of the Unit Level Logistics System-Aviation (ULLS-AE) program in conjunction with their operations in the theater of operations. Support supply and maintenance requisitioning in ULLS-AE and Standard Army Maintenance System-Enhanced (SAMS-E) systems totaling over $5 million monthly.

OPERATIONAL MANAGEMENT AND TECHNICAL SUPPLY GUIDANCE
Troubleshoot and resolve program issues experienced by Logistic Information Systems (LIS) users within the 40th CAB and units operating in 40th CAB area of operations. Provide technical assistance, logistics policy guidance, and effective problem resolutions for information services support personnel, functional users and functional staff.

LOGISTICS SOFTWARE AND SYSTEM SUPPORT
Provide desktop computer support including necessary hardware/software diagnostics for ULLS-AE, SAMS-E and Property Book Unit Supply Enhanced (PBUSE) applications. Provide detailed user instruction for any workstation operating system software or standard application software, supporting training requirements and enhancing personnel expertise. Configure workstation operating system software and all logistics-specific and supply-support application suites.

SUPPLY POLICY ANALYSIS AND RECOMMENDATION
Strengthen relationship within the Chain of Command. Develop relationships with staff and sister companies. Provide critical logistical aviation maintenance support. Administer Apache, Chinook, and Blackhawk helicopter maintenance cycles. Translate periodicity data of prescribed maintenance intervals with aviation maintainers. Track phasebooks and logbooks. Provide unit technical feedback on ULLS-AE, SAMS-E, and PBUSE.

Squad leader, E-5 seeking LEGAL ADMINISTRATIVE SPECIALIST, GS 7

BEFORE: Bulleted List

PROFESSIONAL EXPERIENCE
SQUAD LEADER, E-5   06/2013-06/2016
US Army, Ft. Polk, LA & Ft. Campbell, KY
Logistics Supervisor: 2014-2016

RESPONSIBILTIES:

- Identified, distributed workload and tasks among employees in accordance with established work flow and skill level.
- Resolved simple, informal work complaints of employees and referred others such as formal grievances and appeals to supervisor.
- Served as coach, facilitator, negotiator in coordinating team initiatives
- Built various activities among team members
- Provided input to supervisors' concerning a variety of human resource matters relating to employees including performance, promotions, reassignments, awards, etc.
- Responsible for counseling soldiers monthly, identifying their weaknesses so they can improve, researching and helping them understand the regulations.
- Responsible for identifying the needs for my employees and referring them to social services, or appropriate organization.
- Responsible for soldier's welfare and their families and to research information to solve problems for soldiers and their families.
- Trained 10 team members monitored and reported on the status progress of work.
- Responsible for researching issues for employees and getting back with them in a timely manner with the problem solved.

AFTER: Outline Format

SQUAD LEADER, E-5
06/2013–06/2016
US Army, Ft. Polk, LA & Ft. Campbell, KY
Salary: $52,000
Supervisor: Candice Schreiber, 337-802-9845; may contact
40 hours/week

Coordinate and supervise up to 10 soldiers.

ASSESSING/RESOLVING COMPLAINTS: Resolved simple, informal work complaints and referred others such as formal grievances and appeals to supervisor. Coordinated soldier leave and passes, appointments, orders. Researched information on military skills, job related schools, regulations on dress code, security, and other areas to properly address questions from soldiers and their families. Performed job counseling and progress reports for 10 soldiers monthly.

COMPUTER KNOWLEDGE: Regular, daily use of Microsoft Office 2013/2016, specifically Excel, PowerPoint, and Outlook.

ADMINISTRATIVE SKILLS: Maintained administrative data for 10 soldiers. Prepared daily status reports, PERSTEMPO reports, and soldier evaluations. Coordinated travel arrangements for soldiers on temporary duty assignments. Maintained unit alert roster and social event calendar. Daily distribution of mail. Maintained inventory, turn ins, issues, and accounting records for ammunition in MS Excel. Regularly wrote memos in accordance with regulations. Coordinated missions with other shops. Ordered office supplies.

Key Accomplishments:

- Maintained error-free personnel records and ensured all promotion announcements and orders were delivered on time.

Veterans

For Non-Competitive Hiring Programs (if you are using VRA, Schedule A, 30% or More Disability hiring programs), your resume and cover letter are very important in targeting a specific occupational series. Be sure to study USAJOBS and find positions that match your skills and education, and select a grade level that you can live on. Then write to the appropriate Veterans' Representatives, Schedule A Selective Placement Program Coordinators, or Hiring Managers about your interest in government.

For USAJOBS Competitive applications, your resume should match the Requirements, Qualifications, Specialized Experience, KSAs and the Questionnaire for the announcement. Each position will require specific experience at a certain performance level. This is the way to get Best Qualified.

Spouses

EO 13473 – Priority Placement Program for Spouses (PPP-S), Department of Defense's resume database. Your resume must match Option Codes in the Program S database, as well as the USAJOBS announcement required qualifications. See Option Code sample below.

EO 12568 – Military Spouse Preference (MSP). MSP requires that a spouse candidate be selected before other best qualified candidates. This is optional for the Selecting Official. Resume must match the required qualifications for a specific position. Check off Military Spouse in the USAJOBS Profile.

EO 12721 - Foreign Service family members performing in an overseas mission. This EO can help spouses gain employment with the Federal Government when residing in the United States. The federal resume must match the qualifications for a specific announcement and occupation.

CHAPTER 10

APPENDIX A

OPTION CODES

Series	Series Title	Option Code	Option Title
	Any Appropriate Series	NOA	No Option Applicable
	Any Appropriate GS Series	DAT	Data Transcription
	(see Chapter 10, Section B.6.)	OAA	Office Automation
		STC	Stenography
		TRA	Trainee
		FLP+	Foreign Language Proficiency
		IST	Scientific & Technical Intelligence Production
	Any Appropriate WG Series	TRA	Trainee
018	Safety & Occupational Health	ORB	Ordnance
		MDC	Medical

Source: DOD Priority Placement Program (PPP) Handbook, Defense Civilian Personnel Advisory Service, July 2011, Chapter 10: Option Codes.

Match the Qualifications!

Many transitioning military and spouses will be changing their careers to adapt to the federal job occupations and available positions. In order to write a career change federal resume, find a sample job announcement that is of interest to you.

Find and Study the "Required Qualifications" Section

Your resume MUST match the Required Qualifications in the job announcement. So, you must select job announcements that do not require something highly technical or specific that you simply do not have in your background.

Career Change Sample Case Study

Mariano Tory is a veteran who is changing his career from Helicopter Repairer to Administration in the federal government. Look at his Before and After resumes in this chapter to see how to effectively use keywords to write a career change federal resume.

BEFORE KEYWORDS:
Helicopter Repairer

- ❏ UH-6509 Helicopter Maintainer
- ❏ Supervisor
- ❏ Tool Room Custodian
- ❏ Aviation Ground Support Equipment (AGSES) Technician

> **KNOWLEDGE, SKILLS AND ABILITIES (KSAs):** Your qualifications will be evaluated on the basis of your level of knowledge, skills, abilities and/or competencies in the following areas:
>
> 1. Knowledge of military personnel and administrative policies, procedures, rules, guidelines, publications, etc. Ability to communicate effectively, orally and in writing, using tact and courtesy, and maintain effective work relationships.
>
> 2. Knowledge of mission and unit. Knowledge of support organization functions such as food service, billeting, mortuary affairs, Morale Welfare and Recreation, supply, budget and weapons and ammunition control.
>
> 3. Knowledge of automated systems to update and retrieve information. Knowledge of and ability to use office automation hardware, software, and peripherals.
>
> 4. Knowledge of filing systems.
>
> 5. Knowledge of basic rules of grammar, spelling, capitalization, and punctuation, and standard abbreviations. Ability to analyze products to determine adequacy of program or deficiencies thereof.
>
> 6. Knowledge of official orders preparation, publications, and procedures. Skill of a qualified typist.

AFTER KEYWORDS:
Administrative Specialist

- ❏ ADMINISTRATIVE PROGRAM PLANNING
- ❏ ORAL & WRITTEN COMMUNICATION
- ❏ DOCUMENT PREPARATION AND REVIEW
- ❏ DATA TRACKING AND REPORTING
- ❏ PROJECT SCHEDULING
- ❏ ADMINISTRATIVE AND FINANCIAL SUPPORT
- ❏ TRAINING AND MENTORING
- ❏ PROPERTY ACCOUNTABILITY

Also include accomplishments on administrative and database skills!

Find and study the "Required Qualifications" section.

MARIANO TORY

1234 Hillside Road Leesburg, VA 20176
(703) xxx-xxxx
mariano.tory@email.com

EXPERIENCE

United States Army (USA)
Task Force Comanche, Afghanistan, Operation Enduring Freedom   July 2010 – July 2011

- *Hazardous Materials Certifier* - Certified critical shipping documentation; marked, labeled, packed, and placarded hazardous materials for aerial, vessel, or land shipment as sole certifier of organization; and controlled compatibility of hazardous items transported and security requirements with special attention to U.S. and international laws and regulations
- *Supervisor* - Counseled, trained, and mentored personnel on subject matter performance and event-orientations, special tools utilization, equipment distribution, and accountability; serviced, maintained, and accounted for assigned equipment; and provided support to Command on pre-deployment, deployment, and re-deployment accountability of personnel, equipment, and hazardous materials
- *Tool Room Custodian* - Responsible for property accountability for the Task Force tool room; conducted monthly and quarterly inventories; and provided status reports to the company Commander
- *Tools, Measurement, Diagnostics & Equipment (TMDE) Coordinator* – Monitored projected and delinquent calibration items list; liaised on-site and off-site management of calibrated items; and briefed Task Force Executive Officer
- *Aviation Ground Support Equipment (AGSE) Technician* - Served as the Aviation Ground Support Equipment (AGSE) noncommissioned officer in charge (NCOIC); supervised compliance of AGSE accountability and distribution standards for U.S. Army company; coordinated and filed AGSE inspections, calibrations, repair and maintenance with on and off-site contractors; supported installation fire department with AGSE; and communicated AGSE status reports to Task Force Executive Officer

4th Combat Aviation Brigade, Fort Hood, Texas   July 2009 – October 2011

- *UH-60 Helicopter Maintainer* - Serviced and lubricated aircraft and subsystems and prepared aircraft for inspections and maintenance checks. Conduct scheduled inspections and assists in special inspections. Performed limited maintenance operational checks and assisted in diagnosing and troubleshooting aircraft subsystems using special tools and equipment as required. Used and performed operator maintenance on tools, special tools, and aircraft ground support equipment. Prepared forms and records related to aircraft maintenance.
- *Supervisor* - Counseled, trained, and mentored personnel on subject matter performance and event-orientations, special tools utilization, equipment distribution, and accountability; serviced, maintained, and accounted for assigned equipment; and provided support to Command on pre-deployment, deployment, and re-deployment accountability of personnel and equipment.
- *Tool Room Custodian* - Responsible for property accountability for the Task Force tool room; conducted monthly and quarterly inventories; and provided status reports to the company Commander
- *Aviation Ground Support Equipment (AGSE) Technician* - Served as the Aviation Ground Support Equipment (AGSE) non-commissioned officer in charge (NCOIC); supervised compliance of AGSE accountability and distribution standards for U.S. Army company; coordinated and filed AGSE inspections, calibrations, repair and maintenance with on-post contractors.

Career Change Success: Mariano separated as a 20% disabled veteran (CP), USMC Helicopter Repairer. He did not want to continue in the field of aviation repair. He attended college on the GI bill, got a BS in Philosophy but couldn't find a job with his "before" resume. He changed his resume to the Outline Format and was hired by FEMA!

STEP

6

2nd Combat Aviation Brigade, US Army Garrison Humphreys, South Korea   July 2006 – July 2009

- *Supervisor* - Counseled, trained, and mentored personnel on subject matter performance, military education, and event-orientations
- *UH-60 Helicopter Medical Evacuation Crewmember/Maintainer* - Inspected and maintained 12 UH-60 Helicopters for aero-medical company in South Korea; provided aero-medical evacuation assistance to flight medic; visual guidance to pilots during training missions and real-life evacuation missions; and trained incoming personnel on maintenance, inspection, and flight procedures. Completed 24 real-world medevac missions and received early promotion from Private 1st Class (E-3) to Specialist (E-4)
- *UH-60 Helicopter Maintainer* - Serviced and lubricated aircraft and subsystems and ensured aircraft met inspection and maintenance compliance; performed scheduled inspections and assisted in special inspections, conducted limited maintenance operational checks, diagnosed, and troubleshot aircraft subsystems using special tools and equipment as required; conducted maintenance on tools, special tools, and aircraft ground support equipment and drafted forms and records related to aircraft maintenance.
- *Non-Combatant Evacuation Operations (NEO) Warden* - Participated in Non-Combatant Evacuation Operations (NEO) training exercises for South Korean peninsula; researched documented members' compliance with NEO standards and equipment accountability, and inspected NEO equipment prior to distribution to ensure reliable operations

SKILL SETS

- Spanish (Native or bilingual proficiency), Internet Research, Microsoft Word, PowerPoint, and Outlook, Filing, Editing, Planning, Prioritizing, Proofreading, Scheduling, Teamwork, Transcription, Scheduling, Briefing, Correspondence, Safety, Training, Liaising, Transformational and Ethical Leadership

AWARDS AND ACHIEVEMENTS

United States Army   September 2006 – November 2011

- Army Commendation Medals, Army Achievement Medals, Army Good Conduct Medal, National Defense Service Medal, Korean Defense Service Medal, Afghanistan Campaign Medal (with Service Star), Global War on Terrorism Service Medal, Non-Commissioned Officer Professional Development Ribbon, Army Service Ribbon, Overseas Service Ribbon, NATO Medal, Certificates of Achievement, Aviation Badge; Recommended for promotions (2007, 2008, and 2011), Sikorsky Aircraft Rescue Award

EDUCATION

American Military University   November 2011 – Present

- Bachelor of Arts, Philosophy (Projected to graduate May 2014)
- Concentration in Ethics

AFFILIATIONS

National Society of Collegiate Scholars, VP of Community Services   August 2013 – Present

- Establish and maintain a relationships with local service partners
- Recruit members to participate in service programs and events
- Ensure program compliance with all legal and privacy regulations

Member of: *Student Veterans of America (c.2013), Scroll and Sabre History Club (c.2013), American Philosophical Association (c.2013), Golden Key International Honours Society (c.2013), and 2nd Infantry Division Association (c.2008)*

MARIANO TORY

1234 Hillside Road
Leesburg, VA 20176
(703) xxx-xxxx
mariano.tory@email.com

Work Experience:

S&E Bridge and Scaffold
700 Commercial Ave
Carlstadt, NJ   07072 United States

09/2014 - 12/2014
Salary: 35,000.00 USD Per Year
Hours per week: 50
Logistics and Procurement Specialist
Duties, Accomplishments and Related Skills:

ADMINISTRATIVE & CONTRACT SUPPORT. Support the Director of Operations with contract award and administration for scaffolding, hoisting, and shoring projects. Review and coordinate with other departments and companies to ensure availability of equipment or procurement items. Review and implement procurement requests for the successful completion of contracts. Oversee requisitions and timeliness to increased productivity on project sites. Create and maintain records, memoranda, evaluations, forms, and spreadsheets.

PROJECT COORDINATION. Track and monitor the progress of contracts and purchase orders. Respond to requests for information and confirm system lead times, delivery dates, and costs. Plan and implement improvements to internal and external logistical systems and processes via problem solving. Analyze all aspects of corporate logistics to determine the most cost-effective or efficient means of transporting material or equipment. Conduct environmental audits for logistics activities based on storage, distribution, and transportation.

CUSTOMER SERVICE. Collaborate with other departments to integrate sales, order-management, accounting, shipping logistics, schedule meetings, perform reviews and interviews, and coordinate vehicle repairs and maintenance. Transmit and prioritize approved purchase orders and supporting documents to suppliers, vendors, or internal departments.

Accomplishment:

+ Spearheaded the development of an automated system for initiating action items to department heads. This system allowed for ongoing monitoring of action item status and report creation for executive staff. My efforts in designing, implementing, and maintaining this new system streamlined processes and resulted in a two-day reduction in response times while also increasing deadline compliance.

Supervisor: Kyle Bedlam (345-345-3456)
Okay to contact this Supervisor: Yes

American Military University
N George St, Charles Town, WV 25414
Charles Town, WV   25414 United States

Add your education as a "job block" to fill the period of time.

07/2011 - 05/2014
Hours per week: 30
Graduated - Bachelor's Level Student
Duties, Accomplishments and Related Skills:
Full - time Student with major in Philosophy.

US Army
1001 761st Tank Battalion Ave.
Fort Hood, TX   76544 United States

07/2009 - 10/2011
Salary: 4,500.00 USD Per Month
Hours per week: 40
SGT, 4th Combat Aviation Brigade, Task Force Comanche
Duties, Accomplishments and Related Skills:

ADMINISTRATIVE PROGRAM PLANNING. Composed memoranda for hazardous material transportation, record keeping for equipment and inventories, testing or training courses, and additional duty appointments using Microsoft Word. Created Microsoft Excel spreadsheets to track personnel, equipment, inventory, expiration dates, and procurement status.

ORAL & WRITTEN COMMUNICATION. Evaluated and wrote monthly performance and event counseling on 12 personnel using Lotus Forms viewer. Filed memoranda, performance reports, scheduled inventory and inspection results, and training records. Managed daily and monthly time keeping, coordination, and responsibilities of personnel.

DOCUMENT PREPARATION & REVIEW. Researched nomenclatures and product manuals for procurement of replacement and stock tools, equipment, and parts using Unit Level Logistics System-Aviation (Enhanced); enforced standard operating procedures for unit organization, resources, equipment, and personnel.

DATA TRACKING & REPORTING. Tracked mission-critical equipment using RFID tags and tracking software. Identified overdue items and maintenance schedules. Developed and updated Microsoft Excel spreadsheets for ordering and processing. Controlled compatibility of hazardous items transported and security requirements with special attention to U.S. and international laws and regulations.

PROJECT SCHEDULING. Scheduled hazardous material transportation and composed memoranda to alert constituents, kept detailed records for equipment and inventories, testing or training courses, and additional duty appointments using Microsoft Word. Monitored projected and delinquent calibration items list, liaised on-site and off-site management, and briefed Task Force Executive Officer of test, measurement, and diagnostic equipment status.

ADMINISTRATIVE & FINANCIAL SUPPORT. Created and maintained databases, documents and spreadsheets of procured items, tools, and equipment. Alerted supervisors to financial and material needs. Created Microsoft Excel spreadsheets to track equipment, inventory, acquisition dates, and procurement status.

TRAINING & MENTORING. Supervised, counseled, trained, and mentored personnel on subject matter performance and event-orientations, special tools utilization, equipment distribution, and accountability. Serviced, maintained, and accounted for assigned equipment and provided support to Command on pre-deployment, deployment, and re-deployment accountability of personnel, equipment, and hazardous materials. Ensured financial and personnel readiness.

PROPERTY ACCOUNTABILITY. Responsible for property accountability for the Task Force tool room, conducted monthly and quarterly inventories, and provided status reports to the company Commander. Ensured compliance of Aviation Ground Support Equipment (AGSE) accountability and distribution standards for U.S. Army company.

Accomplishments:

+ Efficiently maintained the command library that consisted of Army Orders, Technical Instructions and Base Instructions. Conducted a major document review to identify relevant and outdated materials. Designed a database for document tracking and automated an audit process to ensure monthly review of all instructions. My efforts led to the elimination of more than 100 outdated instructions.

+ Received an "Outstanding Performance Award" for demonstrating knowledge of the policies and procedures pertaining to contracting and technical publications. Recognized with an "Exceptional Employee Award" for demonstrating an ability to motivate team members and keep projects on track, on schedule, and in regulatory compliance.

Supervisor: Thomas Bundy (123-123-1234)
Okay to contact this Supervisor: Yes

US Army, Pyeongtaek, South Korea
Camp Humphreys
APO, AP   96271 United States

07/2006 - 07/2009
Hours per week: 40
SGT, 2nd Combat Aviation Brigade
Duties, Accomplishments and Related Skills:

SUPERVISION & TEAM LEADERSHIP. Counseled, trained, and mentored personnel on subject matter performance, military education, and event-orientations; ensured financial and personal readiness. Assigned work schedules, evaluated performance, and adjusted resources based on mission needs.

PROCEDURAL KNOWLEDGE. Trained incoming personnel on maintenance, inspection, and flight procedures. Inspected and maintained 12 UH-60 helicopters for aero-medical company. Provided medical assistance to flight medic and visual guidance to pilots during training and real-life evacuation missions. Completed 24 real-world missions and received early promotions from Private 1st Class (E-3) to Specialist (E-4) (2007), and Specialist (E-4) to Sergeant (E-5) (2008).

MAINTENANCE & INSPECTIONS. Serviced and lubricated aircraft and subsystems and ensured aircraft met inspection and maintenance compliance. Performed scheduled inspections and assisted in special inspections, conducted limited maintenance operational checks, diagnosed, and troubleshot aircraft subsystems using special tools and equipment as required. Conducted maintenance on tools, special tools, and aircraft ground support equipment and drafted forms and records related to aircraft maintenance.

Accomplishment:
+ Non-Combatant Evacuation Operations (NEO) Warden - Participated in Non-Combatant Evacuation Operations (NEO) training exercises for South Korean peninsula. Researched documented members' compliance with NEO standards and equipment accountability, and inspected NEO equipment prior to distribution to ensure reliable operations.

Supervisor: Chuck Canoon (234-234-2345)
Okay to contact this Supervisor: Yes

Education:	**American Military University** Charles Town, WV United States

American Military University Charles Town, WV United States
Bachelor's Degree 05/2014
GPA: 3.9 of a maximum 4.0
Credits Earned: 122 Semester hours
Major: Philosophy **Honors:** Cum Laude
Relevant Coursework, Licenses and Certifications:
Proficiency in Writing; Effectiveness in Writing; Research, Analysis, and Writing; International Relations; Social Problems; Social Change; Women of Color: A Cross-Cultural Comparison; Logic; Ethical Theories and Concepts; Contemporary Issues in Philosophy; Enlightenment Philosophy; Modern and Post-modern Philosophy; Ethics in Criminal Justice; Management Ethics; Moral Issues in Health Care; Environmental Ethics; Epistemology; Senior Seminar in Philosophy

MAJOR PROJECTS

PHIL498 Senior Seminar - Philosophy Capstone Course
- The purpose of the senior seminar is to conduct intensive research on a topic of philosophy integrating the knowledge acquired from previous philosophy courses. The research topic was a personal ethic referred to as The Principle of Nonmaleficence, which discusses the state of an initial moral status where one does not inflict evil or do harm to others. The 12-page discourse includes subjects and theories stemming from medical ethics, political philosophy, and environmental ethics.

SOCI403 Social Change – Sociology
- In the course of eight weeks, I partook in a three-stage writing assignment research paper that included structuring a topic; an annotated bibliography; and the full body essay collaborating the causes, patterns, and trends associated with social change. The topic explains how work stigma affects some ways that societies negatively view unemployed, underemployed, and overqualified workers or students from a multidimensional perspective, which includes economic, academic, and cultural ideologies.

WOMS400 Women of Color: A Cross-Cultural Comparison – Women's Studies
- This course examines global women of color from underdeveloped, developing, and developed nations, and various cultural, ethnic, historical, anthropological, and sociological theories and perspectives, which focus on gender inequity and stratification.

Job Related Training:	Technical Transportation of Hazardous Material March 2010

Technical Transportation of Hazardous Material
March 2010

UH-60 Helicopter Repairer Course (15T10)
March 2006 - June 2006

Language Skills:

Language	Spoken	Written	Read
Spanish	Intermediate	Intermediate	Intermediate

Affiliations:

National Society of Collegiate Scholars - VP of Community Services
Student Veterans of America - Member
Second Infantry Division Association - Member
Golden Key International Honor Society - Member

References:

Name	Employer	Title	Phone	Email
Thomas Bundy	US Army	Sergeant First Class	111-111-1111	Thomas.bundy@mail.mil
Chris Wash	United States Army	Staff Sergeant	222-222-2222	c-wash@yahoo.com
Kent Mestnick	Northwest Public University System	Professor	333-333-3333	Kent.mestnick@nw.psys.edu

Additional Information:

AWARDS AND ACHIEVEMENTS
United States Army September 2006 – November 2011
Army Commendation Medals
Army Achievement Medals
Army Good Conduct Medal
National Defense Service Medal
Korean Defense Service Medal
Afghanistan Campaign Medal (with Service Star)
Global War on Terrorism Service Medal
Non-Commissioned Officer Professional Development Ribbon
Army Service Ribbon, Overseas Service Ribbon
NATO Medal
Certificate of Achievement
Aviation Badge; Recommended for promotions (2007, 2008, and 2011)
Sikorsky Aircraft Rescue Award

INTERESTS AND HOBBIES
Information Technology: Diagnosing, troubleshooting, and servicing personal computers by enhancing or installing software, installing or replacing hardware, downloading necessary updates, removing viruses, spyware, and malware; Physical fitness: Running and Calisthenics; Firearm proficiency; Automotive maintenance and performance; Reading; Self-improvement; French language

HIRED!

Kathryn,

Hi! I want to say that I am really enjoying FEMA and am taking full advantage of all opportunities to develop skills and credentialing that they provide. I will be taking a Contracting Officer Representative course in September; I am looking into other courses and classes, as well as training. The pay is good for a GS-09.

Sincerely, Mariano
Feb. 2014 (Began his fed job search Feb. 2013)

Mariano Tory
1234 Hillside Road Leesburg, VA 20176 US
Day Phone: 703-xxx-xxxx; Evening Phone: 703-xxx-xxxx
Email: marianotory@email.com

WORK EXPERIENCE

FEMA
500 C Street SW
Washington DC, DC   20472 United States
04/2015 - Present
Salary: 55,215.00 USD Per Year
Hours per week: 40
Series: 0301 **Pay Plan:** GS **Grade:** 09

Administrative Specialist (This is a federal job)

Duties, Accomplishments and Related Skills:
ADMINISTRATIVE HUMAN RESOURCES SUPPORT. Coordinate and monitor a variety of administrative projects related to human resources (HR). Manage and maintain the FEMA conference room (M1) scheduling appointments, meetings, conferences, invitational events, guest speakers, training exercises and official functions. Primary point of contact to the National Watch Center staff and Director, to include timekeeping, travel coordination, administrative actions and FEMA executive tracking. Assign internal and external requests to appropriate staff members; ensure administrative action deadlines are met. Assist in on-boarding new members by providing educational materials, scheduling meetings and coordinating paperwork and clearances as needed.

PROCUREMENT & ACCOUNTABILITY. Submit procurement requests for office supplies, equipment and services as required. Custodial Officer to the National Watch Center managing 260 sensitive and non-sensitive pieces of agency property, including computer, office and telecommunications equipment, valued at approximately $351K.

ORAL AND WRITTEN COMMUNICATION. Explain non-technical policies and procedures promulgated by OCCHCO and OPM after obtaining clarification from sources. Prepare a variety of material, including correspondence, weekly reports and background material for brief reports, using Inter/Intranet resources, Microsoft Office Suite including Word, Excel, PowerPoint and Outlook.

RECORDS MANAGEMENT. Maintain electronic filing system and hard copy files for administrative programs.

PROGRAM ANALYSIS / PROCESS IMPROVEMENT. Identify and recommend solutions to a wide range of problems relevant to human resources management. Reviews and provides recommendations to the Director on internal operating procedures; and assists in the development and implementation of procedures and processes to expedite, maintain, and continually enhance administrative quality and efficiency. Make recommendations and decisions in establishing priorities among administrative matters requested by various employees or organizations.

Supervisor: Charles Baum (202-xxx-xxxx)
Okay to contact this Supervisor: Yes

Federal Emergency Management Agency (FEMA)
Denver Federal Center
Denver, CO 80225 United States

04/2016 - 07/2016
Salary: 55,215.00 USD Per Year
Hours per week: 40
Tribal Affairs Specialist (This is a federal job)

Duties, Accomplishments and Related Skills:
FEMA EMERGING LEADERS PROGRAM PARTICIPANT for Region VIII, which covers Colorado (regional headquarters), Montana, Utah, Wyoming, North Dakota and South Dakota. Performed rotational assignments as designated.

ADMINISTRATIVE SUPPORT & COMMUNICATION. As Acting Tribal Liaison, monitored and addressed requests for information, calendar invites and tribal-related correspondence on behalf of supervisor during her absence. Prepared communication in response to inquiries from or about tribes in coordination with appropriate leadership. Verified tribal-related publications were stocked for informational distribution. Cross-trained to support other ESF-15 (External Affairs Annex) functions to include daily clips; articles for internal newsletter; FEMA's "Bring Your Child to Work Day" planning; interface and welcoming of staff for international visit from the Emergency Management Coordinator of Mexico; and ensured division accountability to Acting Regional Administrator.

INFORMATION MANAGEMENT / RECORDS MANAGEMENT. Extracted and compiled regional input to prepare senior leadership for meetings with tribal officials. Ensured emergency management information was available on a daily basis for tribal emergency managers, leadership and other federal and local partners.

RESEARCH / ANALYSIS. Conducted high-profile and sensitive in-depth workforce analysis of FEMA Consultation processes across regions and produced a white paper to help identify best practices across the country while also demonstrating gaps. Engaged with Tribal Leadership and Other Federal Agencies regarding best practices for FEMA Tribal relationship building and sustainability of emergency management programs in Indian Country.

SITUATIONAL AWARENESS & COLLABORATION. Maintained current knowledge of changes to tribal leadership, emergency managers (EMs) and issues relevant to emergency management and tribal communities to ensure situational awareness for Region VIII. Reviewed Region VIII's tribe profiles and incident specifics; completed cultural competency research; ensured appropriate coordination with tribal EMs and leadership prior to FEMA staff deploying when an incident occurred. Participated in Regional, National and Interagency Tribal Working Groups; supported National Consultation on Mitigation Planning Review Guidance through collaboration with responsible programs and tribal governments.

Accomplishments:
+ Developed a Records Management system for FEMA Region VIII in the form of a spreadsheet that tracked all tribal consultations from 2014 to present, covering meeting dates/times, preparation time and travel costs. The result was an accurate record and analysis of tribal consultations, which had not previously been recorded.
+ Implemented and adapted Region-wide SharePoint calendar to consolidate division meetings into one location, allowing only meeting attendees to edit their particular meeting entry and enabling authorized parties to create a spreadsheet from the calendar for distribution to state and local shareholders.

Supervisor: Marcia Flowers (303-xxx-xxxx)
Okay to contact this Supervisor: Yes

BOBBI ROBINS

1020 Edmund Ave. • Baltimore, MD 21228
555-555-5555 • bobbir@gmail.com

PROFESSIONAL SUMMARY

Ten years of customer service experience. Continuously awarded highest possible ratings on performance reviews, willing to travel, able to maintain a flexible schedule. Seven years' experience with organizing and disseminating large amounts of data to students, families, Marines, and Sailors. Proficient in Microsoft (MS) Word, MS Excel, MS Outlook, MS PowerPoint, MS Publisher, Naval Correspondence, Adobe Acrobat and SharePoint.

EDUCATION

B.A. (Asian Studies), University of Maryland University College, Okinawa, Japan, 2011
B.A. (Psychology; Human Development Minor), State University of New York College at Geneseo, New York, 2008

WORK AND VOLUNTEER EXPERIENCES

Family Readiness Assistant   Jul 2009 – Present
Marine Corps Family Team Building (Okinawa, Japan and Ft. Meade, MD)
- Volunteered organizational and communication aid to the Family Readiness Officers (FRO) for Combat Logistic Regiment 37, the 31st Marine Expeditionary Unit (MEU), 3d Reconnaissance Battalion and currently Marine Cryptologic Support Battalion.
- Made telephone calls to welcome new families to the unit.
- Assisted with quarterly newsletter for 3d Recon Battalion and monthly newsletters for the MEU.
- Help with the promotion and evaluation of unit events and workshops via spouse-based feedback.
- Assist with administrative duties such as reconciling rosters and service members' documentation.

Lifestyle, Insight, Networking, Knowledge, Skills (L.I.N.K.S). Mentor Feb 2012 – Jun 2013
Marine Corps Family Team Building (Okinawa, Japan)

- Briefed 1-2 assigned sections of the L.I.N.K.S. curriculum at monthly workshops for up to 40 participants.
- Coordinated appropriate activities to accompany oral instruction of L.I.N.K.S. materials.

Family Readiness Officer Nov 2009 – Jan 2013
Marine Corps Family Team Building (Okinawa, Japan)

- Served at the battalion and regimental levels as the Commanding Officer's (CO) representative for Unit, Personal, and Family Readiness Program (UPFRP) outreach.
- Provided support and assistance to Marines, Sailors, and their families through weekly informational email communications and newsletters, monthly target-specific educational workshops, and biannual family events.
- Used MS Excel, MS Outlook, and Marine Online to maintain distribution lists of up to 750 Marines spread throughout up to six companies and their family members; used distribution lists to facilitate home and section visits as well as telephone, post, and email communications in order to maximize awareness of the UPFRP and to connect eligible persons with needed support services.
- Coordinated presence of program resource specialists at major unit events to increase accessibility.
- Conducted biannual surveys to assess needs of families and personnel to increase the program's value.
- Provided the CO with weekly informational updates on the UPFRP via email or brief and hosted monthly Command Team meetings for information dissemination and program activity coordination.

STEP
6

Bobbi is a U.S. Navy military spouse and Program S registrant seeking a career in military transition while her husband is pursuing a U.S. Navy career.

- Interviewed and supervised eleven Family Readiness Assistants and Command Team Advisors as well as coordinated annual volunteer recognitions from the CO and recognition at unit events.
- Utilized various software-based systems, such as SharePoint and resource websites, to gather resource information for inclusion in the weekly email; used MS Word to develop and publish a weekly newsletter that reflected this information and accompanied these emails; built and maintained the unit's eMarine website to serve as an additional reference point for current information.
- Managed annual Unit Family Readiness Funds budgets of up to $17,000, allocated funds and donated items and ensured that spending was within the guidelines stipulated for Non-Appropriated Funds.
- Fostered support systems for new and less experienced FROs through mentorship.
- Created marketing flyers and mailing postcards using MS Word and MS Publisher to promote awareness of targeted unit trainings and gatherings, such as pre-deployment briefs.
- Organized monthly workshops for families in order to increase readiness, resiliency, and to encourage investment in the community.
- Organized quarterly workshops and annual trainings for Marines to increase readiness and improve resource awareness.
- Provided extra support to families during the seven off-island exercises that required participation from the battalion and the regiment via briefs on available services and benefits and extra outreach.

CPR/AED/First Aid/Babysitters' Course Instructor Jul 2011 – Jun 2013
American Red Cross (Okinawa, Japan)

- Taught cardiopulmonary resuscitation (CPR) and basic first aid to adults and teens in monthly classes of up to ten students; also provided instruction on operation of an automated external defibrillator (AED).
- Conducted monthly babysitters' classes for up to 10 teens and pre-teens on how to properly care for infants and children.

English Teacher Jul 2009 – Nov 2012
Y.M.A.K. Institute (Okinawa, Japan)

- Developed lesson plans and conversational dialog examples in order to instruct 15 adult Japanese professionals in weekly conversational English and English grammar classes.
- Established an intensive English course for young adults in transition to overseas employment.
- Prepared monthly quizzes and motivated students to learn and practice English through interaction and discussion. These motivational practices increased student performance on quizzes and their understanding of the English language by 60 percent since July 2009.

Website Administrator and Newsletter Editor Aug 2010 – Jun 2012
Marine Officers' Spouses' Club of Okinawa (Okinawa, Japan)

- Promoted monthly Marine Officers' Spouse's Club of Okinawa events that supported the funding of local charities by updating the Facebook page, the website, and the quarterly newsletter.
- Created, edited, and distributed newsletters using MS Publisher and Homestead web hosting software.
- Obtained member-run business and outside organization advertisements.
- Electronically distributed the quarterly newsletter to more than 300 members of the organization in order to increase participation in club events, present the quarter's charitable donations, and to maximize the amount of time that advertisers had their information on display.

BOBBI ROBINS

1020 Edmund Ave. • Baltimore, MD 21228
555-555-5555 • bobbir@gmail.com
Military Spouse • U.S. Citizen

CAREER OBJECTIVES: Social Services Series, GS-0101-07/09; Administration and Program Series, GS-0301-07/09; Program Management Series, GS-0340-07/09.

SUMMARY OF SKILLS:

Six years' experience in employment readiness counseling, case management, employment training coordination, and database maintenance. Specialized knowledge in federal employment, military spouse and veterans' preference for federal careers. Effective webinar instructor and training coordinator. Effective in customer service, attention to detail and follow-up. Proficient in information databases: Adobe Quickbase, Excel, Google Doc management; gotomeeting.com systems; Constant Contact updates; mail-merge, survey development and study tracking systems.

PROFESSIONAL EXPERIENCE

EMPLOYMENT SERVICES AND TRAINING COORDINATOR   **02/2014 – Present**
Federal Career Training Institute and The Resume Place, Inc., Catonsville, MD   40 Hours per Week
1012 Edmondson Avenue, Catonsville, MD 21228
Supervisor: Kathryn Troutman, (410) 744-4324; may contact

FEDERAL EMPLOYMENT READINESS CONSULTANT: Review client resumes and federal job targets to determine congruence among their eligibility, career goals, and the target job field. Counsel students, private industry clients, current federal employees, military veterans, and spouse clients on their career objectives and direct them towards federal job resources.

CLIENT ASSIGNMENT: Oversee federal resume case management, encompassing a range of clientele seeking consulting, training, and writing services for federal employment. Review client objectives and clarify the scope of work purchased. Evaluate workloads, schedules, and writer specialties to assign projects to 20+ professional staff.

TRAINING COORDINATOR, TEN STEPS TO A FEDERAL JOB®: Coordinate registrations; provide training support, materials delivery for military and university career and employment counselors worldwide.   Follow-up after live and webinar trainings to manage evaluations, materials and Ten Steps material distribution. Produce invoices and discuss Ten Steps training program materials and resources with purchase officers.

WEBINAR INSTRUCTOR: Using gotomeeting.com technology, teach 30-minute webinars to federal applicants, including Ten Steps to a Federal Job™. Coordinate and act as facilitator for webinar series with other panelists. Set up webinar classes online and provide PowerPoints and handouts for webinar classes. Manage course evaluations.

MAINTAIN CLIENT AND TRAINING DATABASES: Using Adobe QuickBase and Excel in Google docs, maintain annual certifications and ensure that registrations and licenses are maintained. For resume service clients, maintain the same database for client information, documents, project estimates and assignments. Follow through to ensure data is up-to-date.

PROJECT MANAGEMENT: Team Leader for a major project aimed at leveraging resources and technology to improve client tracking and success rates. Conduct data analysis across multiple databases and collaborate with staff to revise reporting procedures. Develop customer satisfaction surveys and coordinate ongoing work standardization efforts.

CUSTOMER SERVICE: Deliver high-quality support and service to all customers through effective communication, tactfulness, and a professional demeanor. Provide project cost estimates and interact with clients via phone, email, and other written correspondence. Manage and resolve client complaints, and coordinate with staff members and subcontractors to ensure client satisfaction.

Key Accomplishments:

- Improved communication with past Ten Steps Certified trainers through updated correspondence to support our three year Ten Steps License.
- Supported the creation of a database that tracked the Ten Steps classes being taught worldwide by licensed trainers and the number of classes taught per base. Recognized that more than 226 military bases were licensed to teach Ten Steps to a Federal Job in 2012; and more than 12,000 of the Ten Steps text – Jobseeker's Guide – were supporting the Ten Steps curriculum. Created new data to recognize the importance of federal employment training for military spouses, transitioning military and civilians.
- Improved resume client database system to improve tracking, customer service data and client results information. Designed a survey and received results from 140 federal resume clients.

FAMILY READINESS OFFICER (NF-0301-04)   11/2009 – 02/2013
Marine Corps Community Services, Camp Schwab, Okinawa, Japan   40 Hours per Week
Supervisor: Taylor Sophreti, xxx-xxx-xxxx; may contact

CLIENT SUPPORT & NEEDS ASSESSMENTS: Conducted biannual surveys to assess needs of families and personnel to increase the program's value. Assisted clients in prioritizing issues/developing plans and goals tailored to meet specific needs. Provided support and assistance to the Marines, Sailors, and their families through weekly informational email communications and newsletters.

WORK & FAMILY LIFE EXPERT: Managed the presence of program resource specialists at major unit events to increase accessibility. Fostered support systems for new and less experienced FROs through mentorship. Connected outbound personnel and family members with FROs at their gaining command.

VOLUNTEER RECRUITMENT AND COORDINATION: Interviewed and supervised a team of 11 Family Readiness Assistants and Command Team Advisors. Coordinated annual volunteer recognition events.

COMMUNICATION MANAGEMENT: Used MS Excel, MS Outlook, and Marine Online to maintain distribution lists of up to 750 Marines spread throughout six companies and their family members. Used distribution lists to facilitate home and section visits as well as telephone, post, and email communications to maximize awareness of the program and to connect eligible persons with needed support services.

CONDUCTED INTERVIEWS: Conducted interviews to establish the nature and extent of concerns and issues posed by military family members. Provided assistance in developing personal and family-based goals and plans. Collaborated with social service delivery systems in the military and civilian community to manage clients and ensure positive results.

FINANCIAL MANAGEMENT & ADVICE: Managed annual Unit Family Readiness budgets of up to $17,000. Allocated funds and donated items while ensuring that spending stayed within the guidelines stipulated for Non-Appropriated Funds. Provided the Commander with weekly informational updates on the program's financial status.

NEWSLETTER WRITING & EDITING: Utilized various software-based systems, such as SharePoint and resource websites, to gather information for inclusion in the weekly email. Used MS Word to develop and publish a weekly newsletter. Built and maintained the unit's e-Marine website to serve as an additional reference point.

Key Accomplishments:

- As a Family Readiness Officer at Camp Schwab, Okinawa, Japan, it was my responsibility to coordinate efforts to celebrate the unit's children. I suggested that the children of the local children's home and orphanage, the Nagomi Children's Home in Henoko, come to the Military Family Day. I also coordinated with the American Red Cross to collect items that would be useful to the children in the home, as well as blankets and toys. As a result of my efforts, seventeen children and five caregivers from the children's home participated in the event along with 28 American service and family members. This was the first unit-initiated event of its kind and the first real cultural exchange opportunity for many of the families in attendance.

- Coordinated with FROs across the 3d Marine Division and other outside organizations, such as the Camp Courtney Junior Marines, to plan and execute the first-ever annual 3d Marine Division Marine Corps Birthday Ball for Kids.

VOLUNTEER EXPERIENCE

FAMILY READINESS ASSISTANT (VOLUNTEER)   **07/2009 – 06/2013**
Marine Corps Community Services, Okinawa, Japan   10 Hours per Week
Supervisor: Carl Handers, xxx-xxx-xxxx; may contact

FAMILY READINESS EXPERT: Directly supported and assisted the Family Readiness Officer (FRO) in managing the Unit Family Readiness Program. Applied in-depth knowledge of the Commander's family readiness goals and proactively coordinated with military members and their families to increase morale and quality of life. Advised on military organization, lifestyle issues, and stresses accompanying military life to enhance relationships.

Key Accomplishment:
- Successfully responded to a need for improved communication with Marines and their family members by revamping the design and content of both weekly and monthly newsletters. My efforts directly resulted in a redesigned communication campaign that was buoyed by a visually enhanced publication and a more welcoming tone.

L.I.N.K.S. MENTOR (VOLUNTEER)   **02/2012 – 06/2013**
Marine Corps Community Services, Okinawa, Japan   10 Hours per Week
Supervisor: Bruce Sandtople, xxx-xxx-xxxx; may contact

INDIVIDUAL & TEAM MENTORING: Worked on a one-on-one and team basis to mentor service members and their families on the benefits, resources, and services available. Provided mentorship and guidance across Lifestyle, Insights, Networking, Knowledge, and Skills (LINKS).

CLASS INSTRUCTION: Instructed classes and workshops on a range of topics encompassing the military lifestyle. Delivered information at awareness/briefing sessions and presented key points to specifically targeted audiences, such as parents, children, spouses, etc. Briefed 1-2 assigned sections of the curriculum at monthly workshops of up to 40 participants.

EDUCATION

BACHELOR OF ARTS (B.A.) – 2011
University of Maryland University College
Major: Asian Studies • GPA: 3.82

BACHELOR OF ARTS (B.A.) – 2008
State University of New York at Geneseo
Major: Psychology & Human Development • GPA: 3.34

PROFESSIONAL TRAINING

Certified Federal Job Search Trainer / Certified Federal Career Coach, Federal Career Training Institute,
certified Ten Steps to a Federal Job™ Trainer, June 2013 – June 2016.
L.I.N.K.S. Mentor Training (2012) • Level I Active Military Families Facilitator (2011) • Four Lenses
Facilitator (2011) • SharePoint End User (2010) • Seven Habits of Highly Effective Families (2010)

TECHNICAL SKILLS

Microsoft Office Suite (Word, Excel, PowerPoint, Access) • Statistical Package for Social Sciences
(SPSS) • QuickBooks • QuickBase • SharePoint • e-Marine • Marine Online

SPOUSE PREFERENCE

Spouse of Active Duty USMC. Eligible for consideration under Executive Order 13473, September 11,
2009 Non-competitive Appointment for Certain Military Spouses, and DoD Priority Placement Program.

HIRED!

"Success! I was hired as a Career Coach at a major teaching hospital in
Baltimore, MD. The hiring managers loved my Outline Format with the All
Cap Keywords! Thanks for the encouragement on the new resume!"

If you are a Wounded Warrior, it can be tricky to figure out how to write about your recovery and rehabilitation time in your federal resume. Because each individual utilizes the Wounded Warrior Program in different ways, here are five suggestions on how to include your program activities in your federal resume.

Five Ways to Add a Wounded Warrior "Job Block" into the Federal Resume

1. Include a Short Description

WORK HISTORY:

USMC Wounded Warrior Regiment, West, Camp Pendleton, CA (Feb. 2013 to April 2014) Active Duty, E-5. Completed one year of medical, rehabilitative recovery, reconditioning, counseling and transition training in order to achieve wellness. Achieved a level of success to seek transition into civilian life.

---

2. Include Internships

USMC Wounded Warrior Regiment, West (12/2014 to present)
Active Duty, E-5, Camp Pendleton, CA

- Completed one year of medical, rehabilitative recovery, reconditioning, counseling and transition training in order to achieve wellness. Achieved a level of success to seek transition into civilian life.

- Successfully completed 3 internships while balancing work schedule with medical appointments and clinic visits (physical therapy sessions, and prosthetic related appointments).

HR Intern (September 2014–November 2014)
TriCare, San Diego, CA

SUPPORT HR ACTIVITIES: Attended and contributed to strategy meetings in an effort to refine the existing internship program. Worked closely with the Diversity and Inclusion Manager to share ideas and exchange program information.

Office Clerk/Intern (August 2014–October 2014)
Congressman Clark Kent's Office, San Diego, CA

REPORT GENERATION AND ADMINISTRATIVE SUPPORT: Created and maintained calendars, identifying and resolving any potential scheduling conflicts.

Talent Acquisition & Development Military Program Intern (April 2014–July 2014)
Genuine Education, San Diego, CA

---

3. Show Education and Training

PROFESSIONAL EXPERIENCE

WOUNDED WARRIOR, E-5   **09/2013-Present**
Warrior Transition Unit, Ft. Belvoir, VA   40 hours/week
Supervisor: SSgt Herbie Polo, 555-555-5555, may contact

Undergoing intensive regimen of medical treatment and physical rehabilitation after
suffering service-connected injuries in Iraq, 07/2011. Actively transitioning to civilian life,
including by:
- **Earned cum laude Associate of Science Degree** in General Studies, 2012. Relevant
  courses: Principles of Microeconomics; Introduction to Business; Introduction to
  Computer Applications and Concepts; Math for Liberal Arts; Intercultural
  Communication.
- **Earned Access Data Certified Examiner**, 04/2013; completed 40-hour Digital
  Forensics course.
- **Completed additional Northern Virginia Community College course:** Introduction to
  Geospatial Imaging, 2013.
- **Developing knowledge** of Federal civilian employment process, including resume
  writing, skills translation, job series, application processes, and available employment
  resources.

4. Highlight Transition Skills Training

USCG Wounded Warrior, E-5   09/2014 – Present
Walter Reed National Military Medical Center   Salary: $71.416
Bethesda, Maryland   40 hours / week

WOUNDED WARRIOR REGIMENT: Participate in the Wounded Warrior Regiment which
provides and facilitates assistance to wounded, ill, and injured military attached to or in support of
USCG units, and their family members in order to assist them as they return to duty or transition to
civilian life.

TRANSITION SKILLS DEVELOPMENT: Through comprehensive web-based employment toolbox,
learn about: resume writing, skills translation, networking; transition courses; job placement;
vocational rehabilitation; and specific guidance through the employment process by providing a range
of employment resources and referral information.

KEY ACCOMPLISHMENTS: Learning how to strengthen myself from the inside out through special
programs which show skills in how to improve overall self-esteem, self-confidence, and self-worth.
Fully participate in: leadership, mentorship, lines of operation, individual and unit athletics, and
community service events and activities.

REASON FOR LEAVING: Regained strength and abilities to return to work and life after the
military. Transition date is December 31, 2013. I will be relocating to Bethesda, MD and separating
from the USCG as an E-5 seeking a new career in Investigative Support Services. I am flexible about
the location of my next employment. I am seeking a full-time position.

5. Almost Hidden

FOOD SERVICE SPECIALIST

Dynamic and hard-working food service professional with extensive experience in preparing and serving food, workplace sanitation, menu planning, and customer service. Proven team builder who exhibits decisiveness and leadership under pressure. Demonstrated ability to prioritize tasks and meet deadlines. Excellent public speaking and interpersonal skills. Proven customer service skills with diverse customers. Experience working as a Food Service Specialist for the United States Marine Corps. *Currently in the Wounded Warrior Transition Program, NIH (08/2014 – Present).*

CAREER HISTORY AND HIGHLIGHTS

United States Marine Corps -
2013 – 2014
12th Marine Chow Hall
Camp Hansen, Okinawa, Japan
- **Food Service Specialist**
- Procured, prepared, stored and distributed food for troop consumption.
- Oversaw menu and recipe planning; meal preparation and serving; sanitation; operation and management of facilities and personnel; training; and accounting and reporting functions for garrison and field operations.
- Handled the funding, requisitioning, purchasing, receiving, and accounting for sustenance supplies.
- Provided quality assurance surveillance procedures for food processing, mess hall operations, and storage facilities.

Pursuing Passion Led to Success

"A Wounded Warrior wanted to go into IT, but it wasn't his passion. He was just chasing the dollar. I asked him what he really enjoyed and had experience in. He told me it was dog training. There was a vacancy for that, and he got the job.

"By looking into their passion, the Wounded Warrior can end up doing something that they really enjoy doing. They can stay in the occupation for years to come, because they have a passion for it."

    -- Dennis Eley, MBA, Regional Wounded Warrior Coordinator at the OCHR San Diego Operations Center

The USAJOBS Resume Builder is highly recommended by HR Specialists!

KATHRYN K TROUTMAN
655 West Lake Road
Catonsville, MD 21228 US
Day Phone: 907-333-3333 - Ext:
Email: kathryn@resume-place.com
Availability:

Job Type: Permanent, Temporary, Term
Work Schedule: Full-Time, Part-Time, Shift Work, Intermittent, Job Sharing, Multiple Schedules

Desired locations:

United States - CO - DenverUnited States

Work Experience:

FEMA
1000 Constituation Ave.
Washington DC, DC 20004 United States

01/2013 - Present
Hours per week: 40
INSTRUCTIONAL DESIGN SPECIALIST
Duties, Accomplishments and Related Skills:
CURRICULUM DESIGN AND PLAN LEARNING PRODUCTS: Consult/collaborate enterprise-wide with management, Headquarters, EEO, Safety, Security, Quality Control, Program Specialists, and contractors in the curriculum design, development and maintenance of plans and programs.

ADOBE E-LEARNING SUITE: Utilize Adobe Connect for current virtual training. Collaborate with developers to produce the best quality products.

CAPTIVATE 5: Skilled in using Captivate 5 currently utilizing Captivate 7. Collaborate with developers to produce the best quality products.

DEVELOP COURSE MATERIALS WHICH ARE 508 COMPLIANT: Skilled in applying major principles, theories, and research findings in adult learning including knowledge of evaluation, surveys, tests, and analysis results. Training Emergency Management Specialists in a technical environment allows us to focus on the Adult Learning Theory and Behaviorist theory. According to Malcolm Knowles, adults are practical learners and want relatable information. Coordinate the packaging of training materials and revising or developing new courses based on this process. Manipulate graphics, editing course materials, ensuring instructional materials are 508 compliant.

WEB-BASE COURSE DESIGN AND STRUCTURE CLASSROOM by planning, developing, monitoring, evaluating, delivering, and managing one or more curricula areas utilizing traditional and virtual training. Utilize blended learning in courses. Independently and co-trains courses.

KEY ACCOMPLISHMENTS:

PROFESSIONAL PROGRAM SPECIALIST. Co-Designer/ Co-Trainer. 80 hours to

KSAs, Accomplishments, and Questionnaires

Have you heard that KSAs have been eliminated?
Now they are included in the resume, Questionnaire, and Behavior-Based Interview!

Photo: Hiring Our Heroes Summit, U.S. Chamber of Commerce, Panel Members answer questions and speak to more than 600 military about jobs, careers, and methods to transition after military service, Wheeler AFB, Oahu, HI, Oct. 2016. Partial Panel presentation is posted on YouTube, "How can I go about finding a federal job?" - Kathryn Troutman, 2016 (6 minutes).

It's time to brag! One of the most important parts of a successful federal resume is the description of your major accomplishments at work. USAJOBS announcements usually require specialized experience in a particular area. Many times, they will ask for examples that demonstrate this specialized experience. The best way to demonstrate your specialized experience, and get Best Qualified or Referred to a supervisor, is with accomplishments that prove your excellent performance and value to your organization. It is important to separate your overall duties and responsibilities from your major achievements on the job. Preparing for an interview also requires getting ready to describe job-related accomplishments.

The Office of Personnel Management has a recommended format for writing KSAs and your accomplishments record in a story-telling format: the Context, Challenge, Action, Result (CCAR) Model for writing better KSAs. This CCAR story-telling format is also great for the Behavior-Based Interview.

CONTEXT

The context should include the role you played in this example. Were you a team member, planner, organizer, facilitator, administrator, or coordinator? Also, include your job title at the time and the timeline of the project. You may want to note the name of the project or situation.

CHALLENGE

What was the specific problem that you faced that needed resolution? Describe the challenge of the situation. The problem could be disorganization in the office, new programs that needed to be implemented or supported, a change in management, a major project stalled, or a large conference or meeting being planned. The challenge can be difficult to write about. You can write the challenge last when you are drafting your KSAs.

ACTION

What did you do that made a difference? Did you change the way the office processed information, responded to customers, managed programs? What did you do?

RESULT

What difference did it make? Did this new action save dollars or time? Did it increase accountability and information? Did the team achieve its goals?

Use our free CCAR Accomplishment Builder!

www.resume-place.com/resources/ccar-builder/

KSAs are now included in the federal resume and the Questionnaire with most applications. The Questionnaires are scored based on your answers, and the justification for your answers must be included in your resume.

Vacancy Announcement KSAs

Job Title: CONTRACT SPECIALIST
SERIES & GRADE: GS-1102-05/07

Knowledge, Skills and Abilities:
Possess at least one year of specialized experience performing work of the type listed in the following examples:

- developing, preparing, and presenting terms and conditions in bids or proposals related to the award of contracts;
- or negotiating and **awarding contracts, contract modifications**, and subcontract
- or in legal practice involving the analysis of procurement policies and procedures
- or administering the terms and conditions of contracts
- including such aspects as preparing contract modifications

KSAs Added into the Resume

Director of Logistics-Forward, Rank: Chief Warrant Officer 3
Camp Beuhring, Kuwait

CONTRACT AWARDS - REVIEWED SPECIFICATIONS AND STATEMENT OF WORK: Managed contracts valued at over $660 million. Developed, managed, and provided oversight for the logistical technical work specifications for 300 contractors work performance. Contracts included installation transportation support, field and sustainment maintenance, supply and services, multiclass SSA, retail fuel operations, life support, and food service operations for over 20,000 assigned personnel and over 80,000 US and Coalition Forces deployed to Kuwait, Afghanistan, Jordan, and Egypt.

ACCOMPLISHMENTS:

- Identified and processed for turn-in excess and obsolete equipment that totaled over $10 million for return to Sierra Army Depot saving the United States Army over $8 million in lost equipment.

- Maintained and accounted for over $70 million of Government Organizational Clothing & Individual Equipment (OCIE) in accordance with Army regulations, policies, guidelines, and procedures. Successfully conducted market research on Kuwait laundry service and local office supply stores. Determined which contracts offered best value for available funds.

CONTRACT MODIFICATIONS AND PROBLEM-SOLVING: Conducted an inventory of equipment valued at over $70 million. Recognized the need to modify the contract to accommodate inventory management. Drafted the modification to request modified hours of the warehouse from 7 am - 7 pm to 7 pm - 7 am, so that we could perform the inventory at night rather than in the heat of the summer in over 120 degree weather. Successfully negotiated this modification.

KSA: Ability to collect data and develop database reports

EMPLOYMENT SERVICES AND TRAINING COORDINATOR	02/2014 – Present
The Resume Place, Inc. Catonsville, MD	40 hours/week
Supervisor: Kathryn Troutman, 410-744-4324, may contact	Salary: $45,000

Key Accomplishment:

Supported the creation of a database that tracked the Ten Steps classes being taught worldwide by licensed trainers and the number of classes taught per base. Organized data from several Excel sheets and email records. Worked with a database programmer to create new app for a QuickBase Customer Relations Management System. Created new data to emphasize the importance of federal employment training for military spouses, transitioning military and civilians. Recognized that more than 226 military bases were licensed to teach Ten Steps to a Federal Job® in 2012; and more than 12,000 of the Ten Steps text–*Jobseeker's Guide*–were supporting the Ten Steps curriculum.

KSA: Ability to develop community readiness programs while building coalitions in the location community

FAMILY READINESS OFFICER (NF-0301-04)	11/2009 – 02/2013
Marine Corps Community Services, Camp Schwab, Okinawa, Japan	40 hours/week
Supervisor: Taylor Sophreti, xxx-xxx-xxxx, may contact	Salary: $45,000

Key Accomplishment:

As a Family Readiness Officer at Camp Schwab, Okinawa, Japan, it was my responsibility to coordinate efforts to celebrate the unit's children. Being overseas provided challenges to facilitating such celebrations, as resources were limited and expensive to obtain off-installation. During this time, tensions with the Okinawan populace were very high due to the planned relocation of a Marine Corps Air Station. Recognizing this tension, I suggested that the children of the local children's home and orphanage should be invited onto the base for fun activities with our unit's families. I contacted the camp's Community Liaison and Public Relations Specialist and worked through him to communicate our unit's intent with the leadership at the Nagomi Children's Home in Henoko. I also coordinated with the American Red Cross to collect items that would be useful to the children in the home, as well as blankets and toys. As a result of my efforts, seventeen children and five caregivers from the children's home participated in the event along with 28 American service and family members. This was the first unit-initiated event of its kind and the first real cultural exchange opportunity for many of the families in attendance.

Sometimes after you complete the typical multiple-choice Questionnaire, you might be asked to write narratives to support your Questionnaire answers.

Questionnaire with Narrative Responses (4,000 characters)

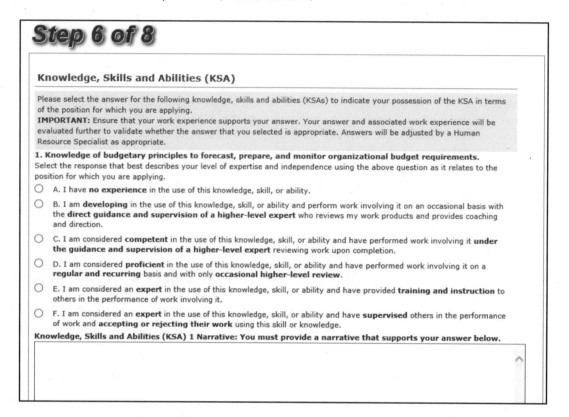

IMPORTANT TIP: You can preview the Occupational or Assessment Questionnaire in USAJOBS! You may need to look for the link in one of the toggle boxes. Here are some examples.

How to Apply —

How to Apply

You are strongly encouraged to read the entire announcement before you submit your application for this position.

To preview questions please click here.

Required Documents —

Required Documents

The documents you are required to submit vary based on whether or not you are eligible for preference in federal employment. A complete description of preference categories and the associated required documents is in the Applicant Checklist (External).

•••

View Occupational Questionnaire, to complete your faxed application

IMPORTANT TIP: You should only apply if you are "expert" qualifed for at least 85% of the multiple choice questions. Explain your answers in your resume.

* 4   [2730] Select the statement that best describes your day-to-day operational experience coordinating management services including personnel management, funds management, and management analysis.

I have not had education, training, or experience in coordinating management services including personnel management, funds management, and management analysis.

I have had education or training coordinating management services including personnel management, funds management, and management analysis, but have not yet used it on the job.

I have experience coordinating management services including personnel management, funds management, and management analysis with close review and assistance from a supervisor, a senior employee, or a senior consultant.

I have experience coordinating management services including personnel management, funds management, and management analysis as a regular part of a job and only in unique or unusual situations did I require assistance or review by a supervisor, senior employee, or senior consultant.

I have experience coordinating management services including personnel management, funds management, and management analysis as a regular part of a job, even in unique or unusual situations. I do not require assistance or review by a supervisor, senior employee or senior consultant.

Others regularly consult me for my expertise and assistance in coordinating management services including personnel management, funds management, and management analysis. I have trained or instructed others on this task or function.

IMPORTANT TIP: This question says, "Check all that apply." Try to check all of them (except "None of the above") if possible.

* 8   [2292] Select the administrative task(s) that you have performed as a regular and recurring part of your job with minimal supervision.

Utilized an automated procurement system to request items/services.

Authorized to make small purchases using a Government Purchase Card Program or similar organizational credit card program.

Verified billing records.

Provided sole source justification to obtain goods and/or services.

Independently searched catalogues, on-line vendors, General Services Administration (GSA) contracts, etc., for the best source of goods and/or services.

Complied statistical data/reports and explained or justified decisions, conclusions, findings or recommendations.

Reviewed program reports to ensure compliance with established formats and inclusion of required information.

None of the above.

Prepare five CCAR accomplishment stories in advance to talk about at the interview.

CCAR Interview Accomplishment Story for Contract Specialist Application - HIRED

Accomplishment Title

Successfully Negotiated and Purchased Army Blues Band New Instruments from Small Retail Business.

Context

I was the Reserves Army Band Leader for the Army National Guard in Baltimore, and in my civilian job I was the Department Manager at Appalachian Blue Grass. I had recently stood up the new Blues Band in order to maintain our musicians, the quality of our performances, and morale of our Soldiers.

Challenge

The challenge was budget for purchasing instruments for the new Blues Band. We needed to purchase the items with a very tight budget, and I was very familiar with this product line. I needed to purchase 16 instruments with a total budget of up to $50K. I wanted to position our small town music shop as the Most Favored Customer for the U.S. Army Band. It was challenging to work with the owner of the small business to negotiate and work with government contracts for instrument products.

Actions

- I researched quality products and negotiated the best prices and availability from vendors and manufacturers through my role as Department Manager.
- I utilized my knowledge of the manufacturers and products in order to build the best instrument inventory possible for the new Blues Band.
- I worked with a Contract Specialist with the U.S. Army to prepare the contracts and manage the competitive bidding for our specialty acoustical instruments.

Results

We successfully purchased $49K in acoustical guitars and electric equipment in just 120 days from a small business for our first Blues Band concert in Camp Liberty, Baghdad. The concert was attended by more than 3,000 civilians and military personnel. Morale was fantastic and it was a great accomplishment for me in that I established the Blues Band and I managed the contracting of the instruments for our expert musicians. The Blues Band is one of the featured bands for the U.S. Army "Pershing's Own" Bands. I successfully managed the purchase of high-quality acoustical guitars, banjos, dobros and electric instruments for a new Blues Band and other band features with the small retail business, which became a Small Set-Aside Business / GSA contractor and vendor for the U.S. Army Bands.

Use our free CCAR Accomplishment Builder!

www.resume-place.com/resources/ccar-builder/

Cover letters are usually optional.
Read the vacancy announcement instructions!

Specialized Experience

Add a list of skills and experience that you can offer that matches the specialized experience in the announcement.

Compelling

Tell the reader why you are an excellent candidate and you believe in their mission.

Passion and Interest in the Mission

Write about your interest in the mission of the agency or organization. If you know the mission and can speak about it in a sentence, you can stand out above your competition.

Why Hire Me?

Be sure to mention your best qualities (that match the announcement).

Letter of Interest

The cover letter is more than a transmittal. The cover letter is a letter of interest; you are interested in the job. Take this opportunity to sell your special qualifications, certifications, training, and mission-related experiences. This is another small writing test.

Uploading a Short Cover Letter into USAJOBS or Adding It to the Builder

With USAJOBS, you can add the letter into Additional Information section. With Application Manager, you can upload your cover letter from your USAJOBS account.

Special Considerations

You can mention your willingness to relocate, eligibility for non-competitive spouse appointments, veterans' preference, reasons for wanting to move, such as family, and other special interest items in the cover letter.

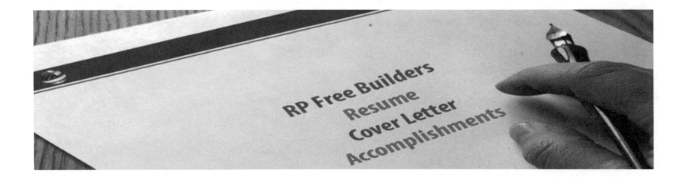

Use our free Cover Letter Builder!

www.resume-place.com/resources/cover-letter-builder/

Cover letters for federal jobs are usually NOT required, but you can send a cover letter along with your federal resume for the supervisor, if your resume is referred to a supervisor. Be sure to include: your specialized experience related to the position; significant education or training; and a top accomplishment that can be impressive. Add details about your job search, such as your interest in a specific geographic area. Include a sentence about your interest in the mission of the agency.

This sample was created using our Cover Letter Builder: www.resume-place.com/resources/cover-letter-builder/

JOHN SMITH
1000 Smith Avenue | Ft. McCoy, WI 90210
444-444-4444 | john.smith@netflix.com

June 5, 2015

Department Name
Division Name
Address Line 1
Address Line 2

RE: USAJOBS Announcement #: XXX-XXXX-XXX

To Whom It May Concern:
Please accept my resume and supporting materials in application for the Geospatial Analyst position with National Geospatial Intelligence Agency (NGA) (USAJOBS Announcement #: XXX-XXXX-XXX). My relevant experience for the position includes:

- Three years of experience in military geospatial intelligence environments with in-depth experience in map design, map production, and geospatial intelligence support.
- I have collaborated with entities such as U.S. Central Command, U.S. Cyber Command, and the Intelligence Community.
- I am a subject matter expert in cartography, including 3D modeling, and am fluent in the use of geospatial analysis and mapping software.

I believe that I would be an asset to your organization because:

- I have delivered high-quality geospatial support for several agencies within the Intelligence Community. I possess overseas military experience, including in support of active combat operations in the Middle East.
- My military record demonstrates that I am a skilled analyst and briefer with substantial real-world experience. I am known for my ability to communicate, to pull long hours, and for my precision in overseeing collection and mapping efforts.
- I am committed to providing rapid analyses and quality recommendations regardless of situational complexity. I will bring those skill sets and problem solving qualities to bear on NGA's challenges.

Thank you for your time and consideration. I look forward to your response.

Sincerely,
John Smith

Enclosures: Resume, DD-214

Troy S. Yates
2220 Marcos Ave.
San Marcos, California 92078
E-mail: Troy.s.yates@gmail.com
Home Phone: 888-888-8888
Work Phone: 888-888-8888

12/20/20xx

Rodney Leonard, Veteran's Representative
Department of Homeland Security
Vets@dhs.gov

Dear Mr. Leonard,

Please find enclosed my Federal Resume for the DHS positions in the areas of:
Logistics Management Specialist, Emergency Management Specialist, Program
Analysis and/or Administrative Officer. I would like to be considered for GS-11 or 12
positions. I am qualified for VRA, 30% or more Disabled, and Schedule A hiring
programs.

My relevant experience for the above positions includes:
- 23 years of experience serving as an Officer in the U.S. Air Force. I was
  promoted to and served for 5 years in the top 4 percent of the entire U.S. Air
  Force total force structure. Uncompromising ethics and trustworthiness have
  been the cornerstones of my career.
- I have extensive experience as a Squadron Commander (Director) leading,
  managing, and overseeing the activities and operations of large, dynamic, and
  progressive organizations.
- As the Chief of Mission Assurance for the U.S. Air Force in the Pentagon,
  Washington DC, I'm experienced with senior level staff work developing and
  implementing policy requiring a collaborative, diplomatic, and a political mindset.

I believe that I would be an asset to your organization because:
- I am highly detailed and bring an extensive knowledge of the principles and
  practices of supervision, organizational management, budgeting, administration,
  and personnel management.
- As a Servant Leader, I would develop and maintain a good-natured and
  engaging work environment for both the staff and community.

Sincerely,
Troy S. Yates

Enclosures: DD-214, VA Letter and Schedule A Letter; 4-page Federal Resume

Apply for Jobs with USAJOBS

PART 1: Get ready on USAJOBS with your profile, resume, and documents.

PART 2: Apply for federal positions with the Questionnaire and SUBMIT.

Photo: Kathryn Troutman, Author, Jobseeker's Guide, teaches USAJOBS search to military personnel at Schofield Barracks, Army Community Services, Oahu, H[...] October 2016.

2016
FEDERAL JOB SEMINAR

SPECIAL TWO-PART SEMINAR ON MASTERING
THE FEDERAL APPLICATION PROCESS FOR ALL
FEDERAL JOB SEEKERS AND PRIORITY PLACEMENT
PROGRAM FOR MILITARY SPOUSES (PPP-S)

Before you begin applying for jobs in USAJOBS, it's important to set up your account and profile correctly first. Here's how.

Logging In: Write Down Your Password!

Record your password!

Use a personal email account instead of a work email account.

USAJOBS Account Home

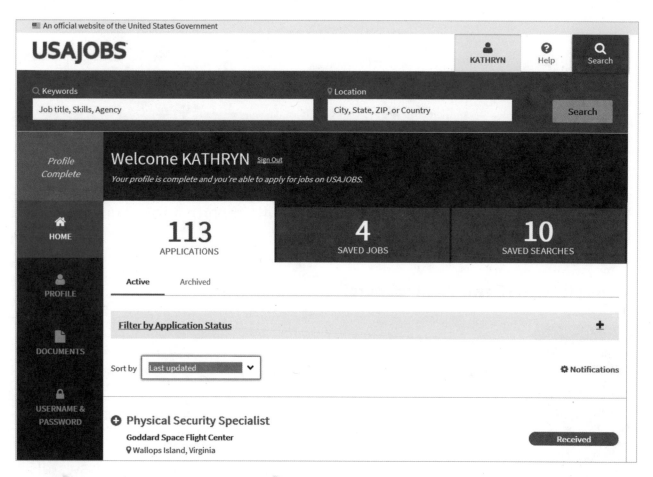

Account actions

View your applications, saved jobs, and saved searches

Application status information

Your Applications

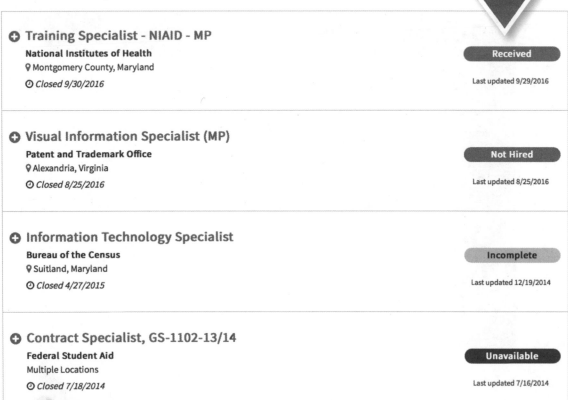

Click on one of these applications to see more information

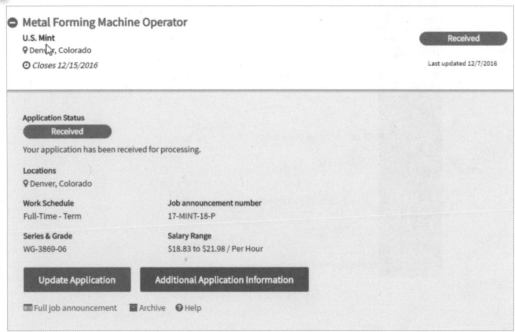

Saved Jobs

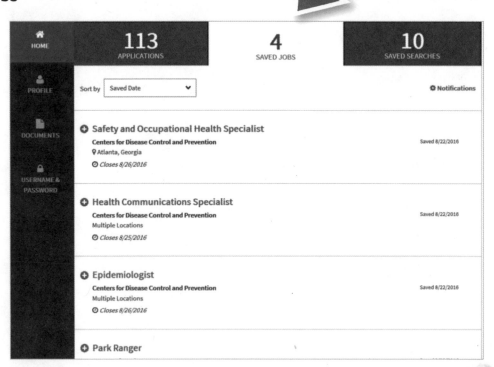

Saved Searches

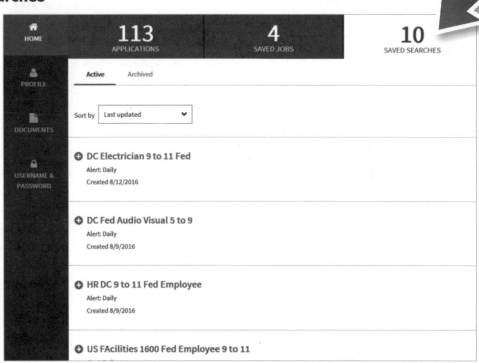

Profile

Answer the profile sections carefully!

Your SSN will not be required in USAJOBS, but you might have to add your SSN and DOB into the Questionnaire application system.

Profile > Eligibility > U.S. Citizenship

Profile > Eligibility for Veterans' Preference

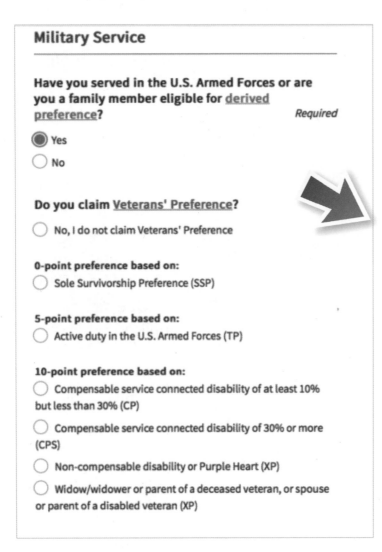

Eligibility Documentation: Make sure you upload in the documents section!

DD-214, SF-15, SF-50, PCS Orders, etc.

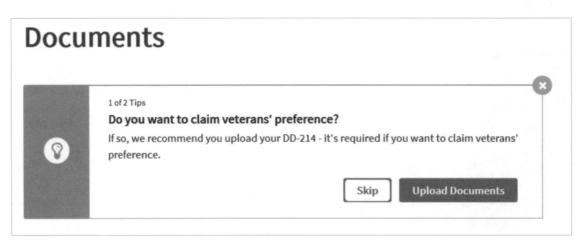

Do you claim Veterans' Preference?

◯ No, I do not claim Veterans' Preference

0-point preference based on:

◯ Sole Survivorship Preference (SSP)

5-point preference based on:

◯ Active duty in the U.S. Armed Forces (TP)

10-point preference based on:

◯ Compensable service connected disability of at least 10% but less than 30% (CP)

◯ Compensable service connected disability of 30% or more (CPS)

◯ Non-compensable disability or Purple Heart (XP)

◯ Widow/widower or parent of a deceased veteran, or spouse or parent of a disabled veteran (XP)

Are you a veteran who was separated from the armed forces under honorable conditions after completing an initial continuous tour of duty of at least 3 years (may have been released just short of 3 years) (VEOA)?

◯ Yes

◯ No

Military Service Dates

Start

Month	Day	Year

For example: 03 18 2010

End

Month	Day	Year

☐ Future/To-be-determined Release Date

For military members with a separation date in the near future, please enter the Start Date and select the Future/To-be-determined Release Date checkbox. If you have a break in service, please add your additional service dates.

[Add Service Dates]

Profile > More Eligibility Questions

Federal Employment

Please select the statement below which best reflects your federal employment status (if applicable). *Required*

◯ I am not and have never been a federal civilian employee.

◯ I am currently a federal civilian employee.

◉ I am a former federal civilian employee with reinstatement eligibility.

◯ I am a former federal civilian employee but do not have reinstatement eligibility.

Are you a current federal civilian employee serving under a Veterans' Recruitment Appointment (VRA)?

◯ Yes

◉ No

Indicate the pay plan, series, grade level/pay band of the highest permanent graded position you ever held as a Federal Civilian Employee. (Question does Not apply to members of the armed forces covered under Title 10.)

Pay Plan

GS General Schedule (Ch. 51, 5 U.S.C.) ⌄

Occupational Series

0819 Environmental Engineering ⌄

Highest Pay Grade

13

Are you a retiree receiving a Federal annuity?

◯ Yes

◉ No

Have you accepted a buyout from a Federal agency within the past 5 years?

◯ Yes

◉ No

Profile > Preferences > Unique Hiring Paths

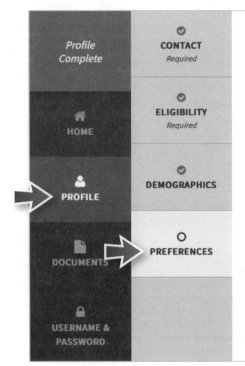

Profile

Preferences

All fields are optional

The following questions are optional. This information is used if your resume is searchable. If you've made your resume searchable, this information helps agencies match your work preferences with the job opportunities they're looking to fill. Learn how to make your resume searchable.

Travel & Rel...

Are you willing...

○ Yes

○ No

Unique Hiring Paths

Do you fall into one of the groups listed below? If yes, you may be eligible to apply for certain jobs or receive preference through a unique hiring authority.

Agencies use this information to search for potential applicants to hire under one of these special hiring authorities. This information is optional. Whether you choose to provide this information, or not, does not impact your application or your ability to apply to a job under a special hiring authority. Learn more about unique hiring paths.

Veterans

☐ Veterans Recruitment Appointment (VRA)

☐ 30% Or More Disabled Veteran

☐ Disabled veterans who have completed a VA training program

Military Spouses

☐ Military Spouse

Certain former overseas employees

☐ Certain former overseas employees

Individuals with Disabilities

☐ Schedule A Disabled

More information about special hiring authorities here:

www.usajobs.gov/Help/working-in-government/unique-hiring-paths/

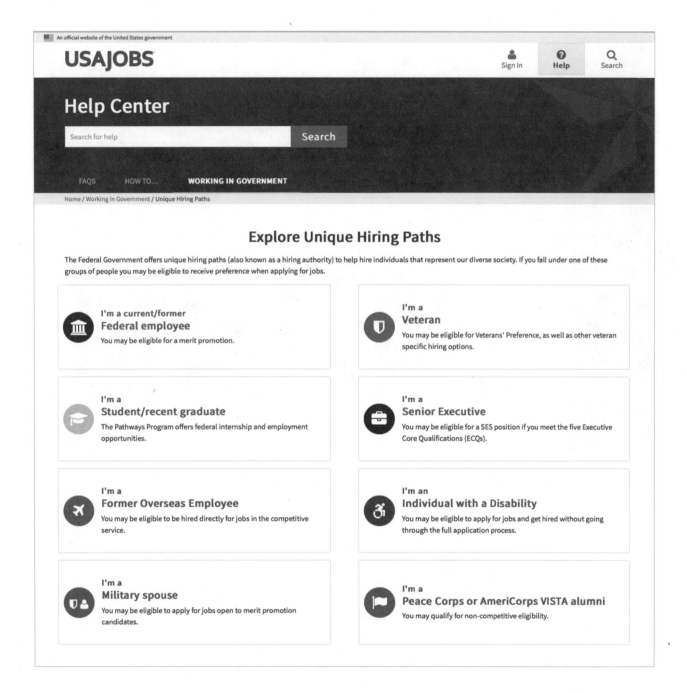

Documents > Resumes

Build or Upload Your Resumes into USAJOBS
You can store 5 resumes at a time.

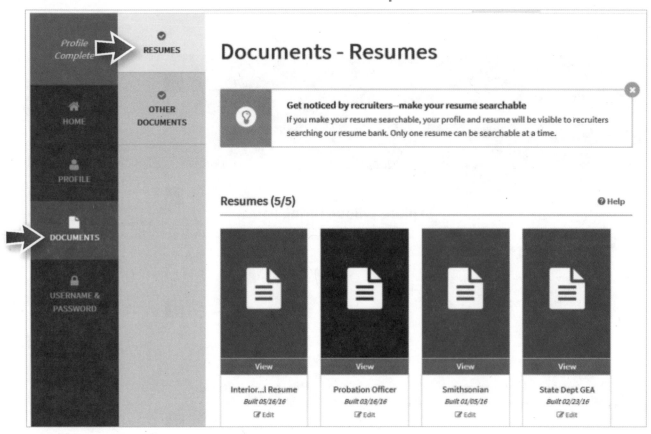

You will have the option to UPLOAD a resume from your computer or BUILD a resume using the resume builder.
Which one should you choose?

See page 152!

Documents > Other Documents

Include ALL of the requested documents!

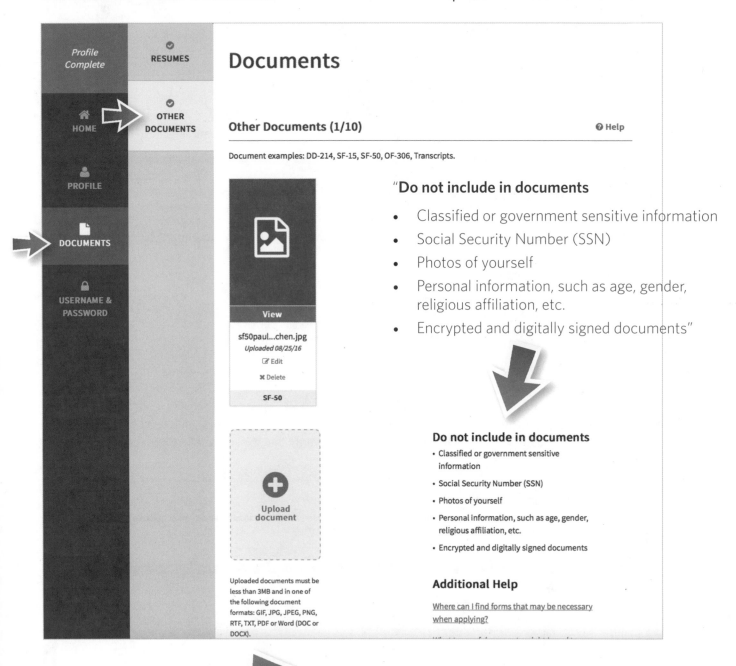

Documents

Other Documents (1/10) ⊘ Help

Document examples: DD-214, SF-15, SF-50, OF-306, Transcripts.

View

sf50paul...chen.jpg
Uploaded 08/25/16
✎ Edit
✖ Delete

SF-50

Upload document

Uploaded documents must be less than 3MB and in one of the following document formats: GIF, JPG, JPEG, PNG, RTF, TXT, PDF or Word (DOC or DOCX).

"**Do not include in documents**

- Classified or government sensitive information
- Social Security Number (SSN)
- Photos of yourself
- Personal information, such as age, gender, religious affiliation, etc.
- Encrypted and digitally signed documents"

Do not include in documents

- Classified or government sensitive information
- Social Security Number (SSN)
- Photos of yourself
- Personal information, such as age, gender, religious affiliation, etc.
- Encrypted and digitally signed documents

Additional Help

Where can I find forms that may be necessary when applying?

"Uploaded documents must be less than 3MB and in one of the following document formats: GIF, JPG, JPEG, PNG, RTF, TXT, PDF or Word (DOC or DOCX)."

The Great Debate: Resume Builder vs. Upload

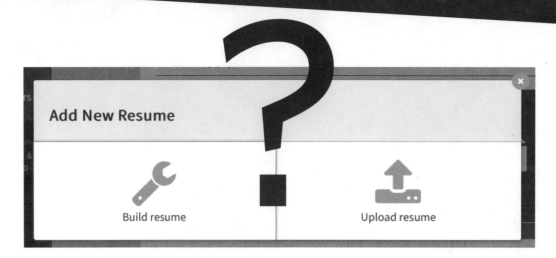

BEGINNER: Are you new to USAJOBS? Use the builder!

For first-time federal jobseekers, I highly recommend the builder. For each work experience block, the builder prompts you to enter:

- Month and year to month and year*
- Hours per week*
- Supervisor name and phone (if available)
- Can HR contact this person (if contact info is provided)?
- Employer name*
- Employer street address*
- Employer city, state, zip code*

The information with an asterisk is REQUIRED, and you will not be considered for a job if that information is missing from your resume. The USAJOBS resume builder will verify that this information is in your resume (see screenshot below).

> **!** **Action Required**
> You are not able to apply because your selected resume is missing necessary fields. You can edit your resume or upload a new resume to continue your application submission.

The builder gives step-by-step instructions for creating your resume. You can start and stop anytime and print out your resume for review.

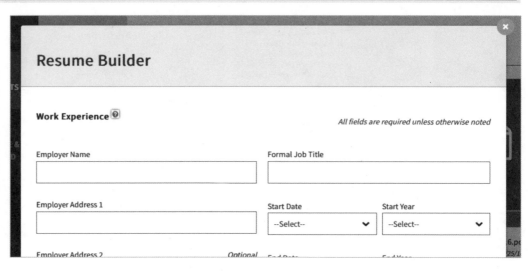

ADVANCED: USAJOBS Resume Upload for Advanced Federal Jobseekers

If you are an experienced federal jobseeker and your resume contains all required information, you can go into your account and PREVIEW your BUILDER RESUME. Then you can copy and paste it into a Word file and edit that file to build a better-looking federal resume.

There are several things you can do with an uploaded resume that are not permitted within the strict format of the USAJOBS resume builder. You can add to the top of an uploaded resume a Profile of experience. You can feature certain important relevant certifications, technical skills, accomplishments, and honors. You can pull out and highlight certain information that you cannot feature in the builder format.

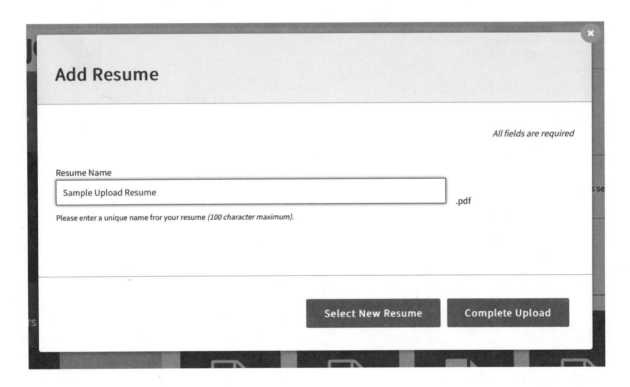

Environmental Protection Agency
1200 Pennsylvania Avenue, NW
Washington DC, DC 20460 United States

07/2013 - Present
Hours per week: 40
Series: 0819 **Pay Plan:** GS **Grade:** 13
Environmental Engineer (This is a federal job)
Duties, Accomplishments and Related Skills:
EFFECTIVE COMMUNICATIONS TO PROTECT PUBLIC HEALTH: As team lead and

NEW TIP: When using a Mac, do not use Preview to create a PDF of your resume for uploading. There are known issues. Highly recommended: Check your document in Adobe Reader (not Adobe Acrobat) prior to uploading.

Time to actually apply for a job!

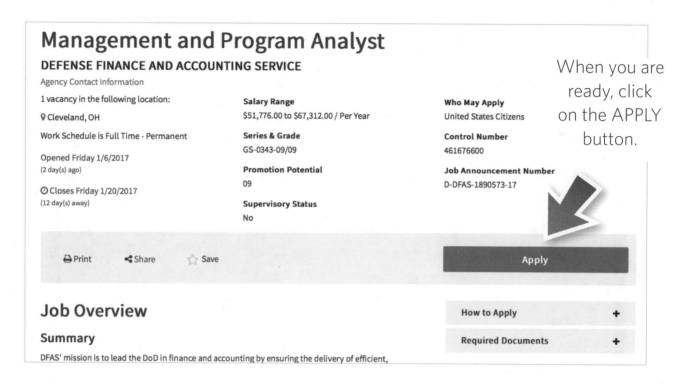

You will then go through five steps in USAJOBS to create your application, after which you will have to go to another site to complete your Questionnaire and application.

In USAJOBS:

1. Select resume (easy if you name your resumes appropriately!)
2. Select documents (easy if they are already uploaded)
3. Review package
4. Include personal info
5. Continue application with agency

Select Resume: Easy if you name your resumes appropriately!

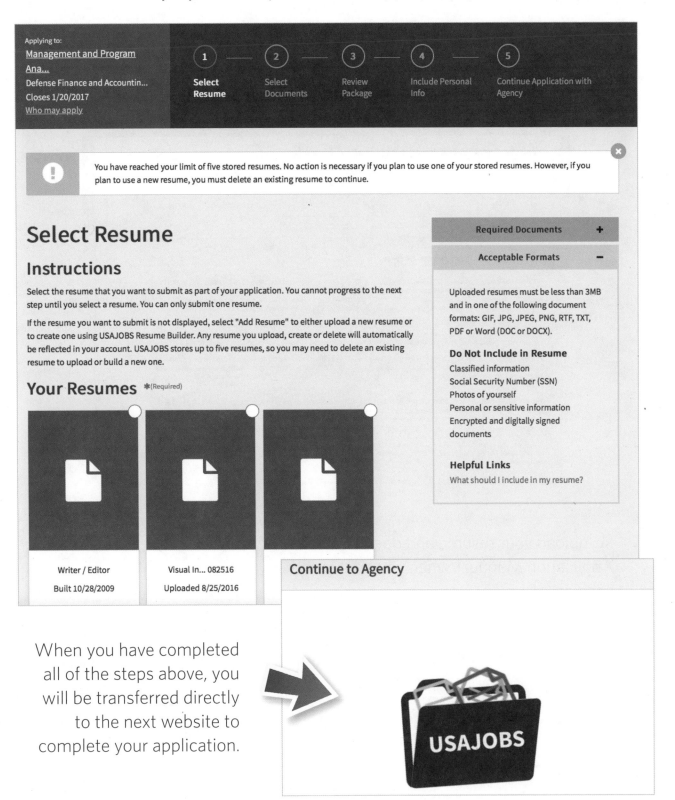

Applying to:
Management and Program Ana...
Defense Finance and Accountin...
Closes 1/20/2017
Who may apply

1 — 2 — 3 — 4 — 5

Select Resume | Select Documents | Review Package | Include Personal Info | Continue Application with Agency

You have reached your limit of five stored resumes. No action is necessary if you plan to use one of your stored resumes. However, if you plan to use a new resume, you must delete an existing resume to continue.

Select Resume

Instructions

Select the resume that you want to submit as part of your application. You cannot progress to the next step until you select a resume. You can only submit one resume.

If the resume you want to submit is not displayed, select "Add Resume" to either upload a new resume or to create one using USAJOBS Resume Builder. Any resume you upload, create or delete will automatically be reflected in your account. USAJOBS stores up to five resumes, so you may need to delete an existing resume to upload or build a new one.

Your Resumes ✱(Required)

Writer / Editor
Built 10/28/2009

Visual In... 082516
Uploaded 8/25/2016

Required Documents +

Acceptable Formats –

Uploaded resumes must be less than 3MB and in one of the following document formats: GIF, JPG, JPEG, PNG, RTF, TXT, PDF or Word (DOC or DOCX).

Do Not Include in Resume
Classified information
Social Security Number (SSN)
Photos of yourself
Personal or sensitive information
Encrypted and digitally signed documents

Helpful Links
What should I include in my resume?

Continue to Agency

When you have completed all of the steps above, you will be transferred directly to the next website to complete your application.

USAJOBS

Application Manager

The most common Automated Recruitement System (ARS) website you could be transferred to is Application Manager to complete your application. The Questionnaires are basically similar among the different systems and will usually include multiple choice and self-assessment style questions.

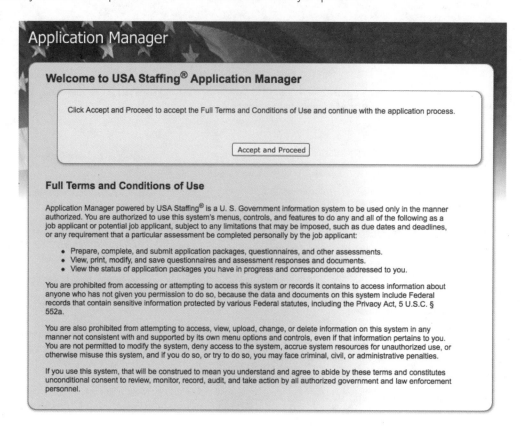

- Re-upload your resume and documents in Application Manager when you apply for the position.

- Give yourself all the credit you can on the self-assessment questions and back up your answers in your resume.

- Be sure to click the final button "Submit My Answers" or your application will not be submitted.

Examples of Other Automated Recruitment Systems for Completing Your Application

Monster.com (Transportation Security Administration)

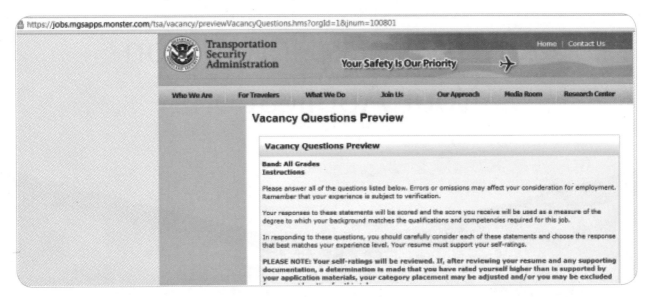

USAStaffing (U.S. Customs and Border Protection)

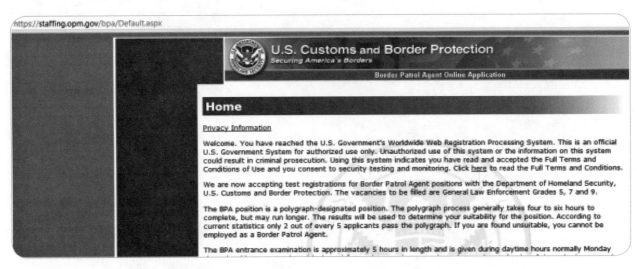

STEP

9

Track and Follow Up on Your Applications

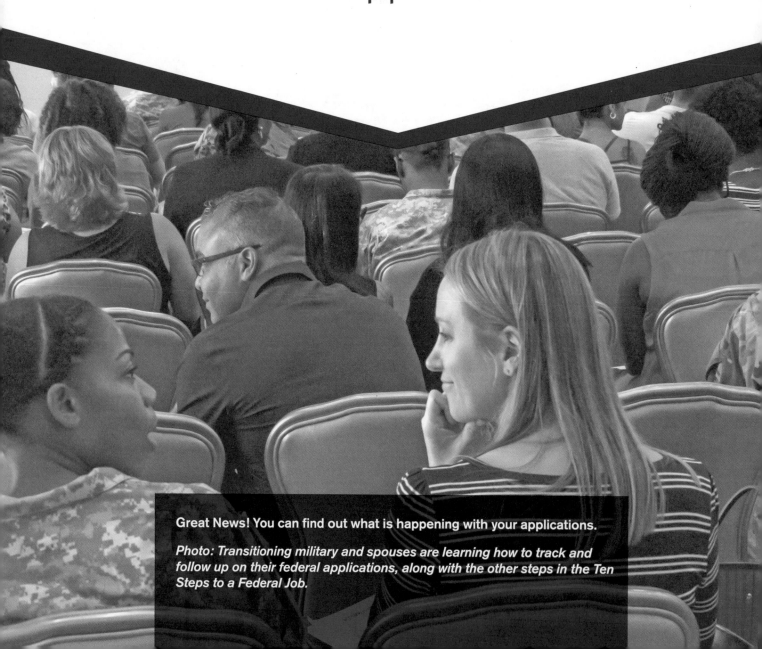

Great News! You can find out what is happening with your applications.

Photo: Transitioning military and spouses are learning how to track and follow up on their federal applications, along with the other steps in the Ten Steps to a Federal Job.

USAJOBS

Check the status of your application on your account home page on USAJOBS.

By Email

You may also receive your application results by email.

When to Call HR

You can call HR to find out what happened to your application if you haven't heard anything two to three weeks past the closing date. Many HR specialists respond to phone messages.

Sample Telephone Message Script

"Hello, I'm Kathryn Troutman. I'm calling regarding my application submitted for announcement number 10505 for Writer-Editor, GS-12. The closing date was 3/31 and I'm checking on the status of the recruitment. I can be reached at 410-744-4324 from 9 until 5, Monday through Friday, Eastern Standard Time. If you get voicemail, you can leave a message regarding the position. Thank you for your time. I look forward to your information."

Emails from Human Resources

If you receive an email from the HR specialist concerning your qualifications for the position and you can't understand the email, just write back or call to get clarification of the email.

Emailing the HR Representative

If there is an email address on the announcement, you could try contacting the human resources specialist by email. You can contact the HR specialist to check on the status of your applications and find out your application score if this information is not posted online. Here is a sample letter:

Subject line: Status of announcement 10101

Dear Ms. Jones,

I submitted my Federal resume, KSAs, and evaluation for the position of Writer-Editor, announcement no. 10101 on Dec. 22 by USPS. I'd like to check the status of my application and the recruitment, please.

Is it still open and was I found qualified? Thank you very much for your time.

Sincerely,

Kathryn Troutman

Daytime phone: 410-744-4324 (M-F, 9- 5 EST) messages okay

Your Applications

Application status information

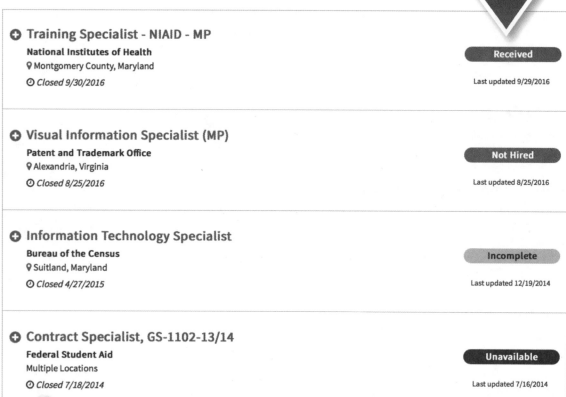

Training Specialist - NIAID - MP
National Institutes of Health
♀ Montgomery County, Maryland
⏲ *Closed 9/30/2016*

Received
Last updated 9/29/2016

Visual Information Specialist (MP)
Patent and Trademark Office
♀ Alexandria, Virginia
⏲ *Closed 8/25/2016*

Not Hired
Last updated 8/25/2016

Information Technology Specialist
Bureau of the Census
♀ Suitland, Maryland
⏲ *Closed 4/27/2015*

Incomplete
Last updated 12/19/2014

Contract Specialist, GS-1102-13/14
Federal Student Aid
Multiple Locations
⏲ *Closed 7/18/2014*

Unavailable
Last updated 7/16/2014

Click on one of these applications to see more information

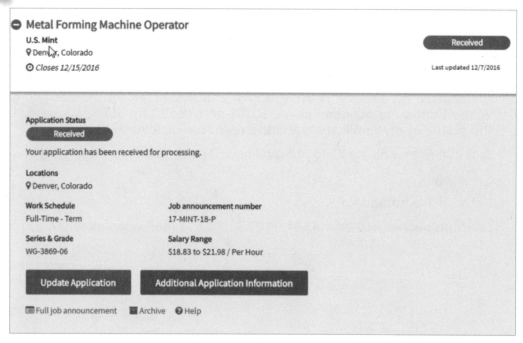

Metal Forming Machine Operator
U.S. Mint
♀ Denver, Colorado
⏲ *Closes 12/15/2016*

Received
Last updated 12/7/2016

Application Status

Received

Your application has been received for processing.

Locations
♀ Denver, Colorado

Work Schedule
Full-Time - Term

Job announcement number
17-MINT-18-P

Series & Grade
WG-3869-06

Salary Range
$18.83 to $21.98 / Per Hour

Update Application   Additional Application Information

📧 Full job announcement   🗄 Archive   ❓ Help

Find out what happened with your applications! If the news isn't great, change your resume or questionnaire answers! The types of results you could receive about your application could be: Incomplete, Not Eligible, Eligible, Best Qualified, Best Qualified and Not Among the Most Qualified to be Referred, Best Qualified and Referred. It's important to check your Notice of Results (NORs), so that you can gauge the success of your applications.

Not among the Best Qualified and not referred

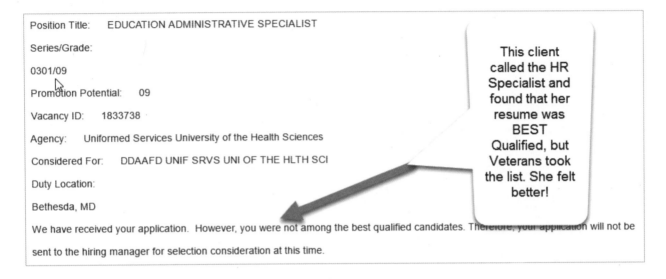

Resume and questionnaire qualified, but rating fell below the cutoff score and not referred.

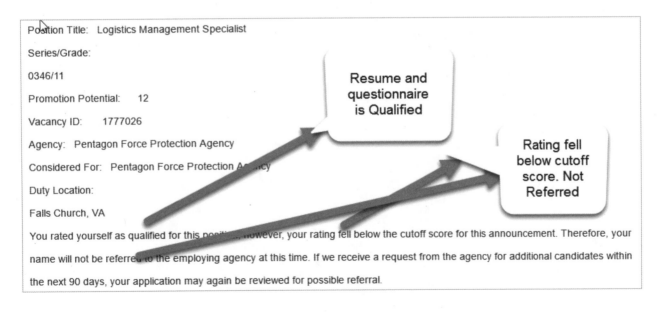

Not among the most highly qualified candidates and not referred

Position Title: Eligibility Specialist

Series/Grade:

0301/09

Vacancy ID: 1752585

Agency: Office of the Secretary of the Army

Considered For: W1C9AA Arlington National Cemetery

Duty Location:

Arlington, VA

We have reviewed your application and found you qualified for the position listed above. However, you were not among the most highly qualified candidates. Therefore, your name will not be referred to the employing agency at this time. If we receive a request from the agency for additional candidates, or another agency requests a list of eligibles for a very similar position within the next 90 days, your application will again be reviewed for possible referral.

Thank you for your interest in Department of Army employment.

Not Referred

Not "among the most qualified candidates"

Referred!

Referral Type: Current or former employees with Federal Civil Service status or VEOA candidates

Referral Name: WE-17-MPP-23837S0

Status: R - Referred

Vet Pref: NV (Clm)

Locations:

Montgomery County, MD

Referred is a GREAT RESULT!

BEST QUALIFIED, REFERRED, INTERVIEWED, AND HIRED!

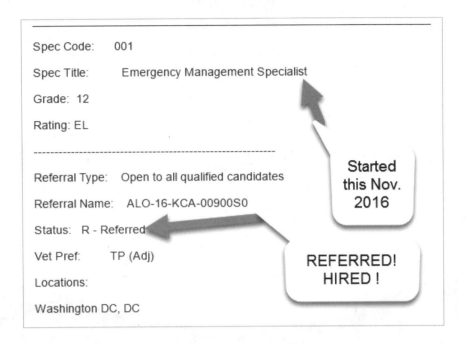

Spec Code: 001

Spec Title: Emergency Management Specialist

Grade: 12

Rating: EL

Referral Type: Open to all qualified candidates

Referral Name: ALO-16-KCA-00900S0

Status: R - Referred

Vet Pref: TP (Adj)

Locations:

Washington DC, DC

Started this Nov. 2016

REFERRED! HIRED !

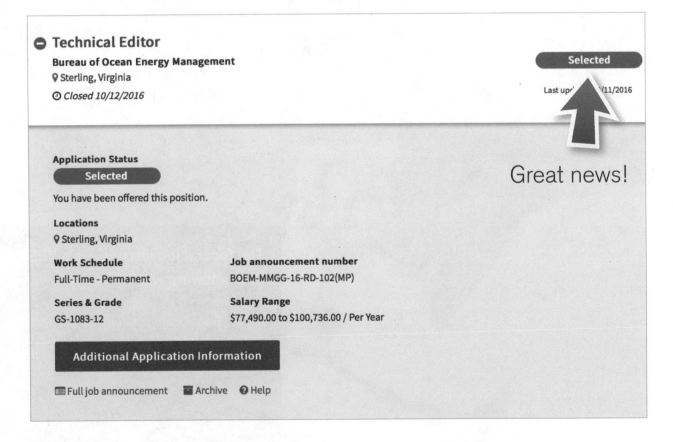

⊖ Technical Editor

Bureau of Ocean Energy Management

📍 Sterling, Virginia

🕐 *Closed 10/12/2016*

Selected

Last up... .../11/2016

Great news!

Application Status

Selected

You have been offered this position.

Locations

📍 Sterling, Virginia

Work Schedule

Full-Time - Permanent

Job announcement number

BOEM-MMGG-16-RD-102(MP)

Series & Grade

GS-1083-12

Salary Range

$77,490.00 to $100,736.00 / Per Year

Additional Application Information

📖 Full job announcement   ✉ Archive   ❓ Help

STEP

10

Interview for a Federal Job

The federal job interview is a TEST. Your answers will be graded!

Photo: Transitioning military personnel discussing federal resumes and USAJOBS applications with Kathryn Troutman at the Hiring our Heroes Summit, October 2016

Be prepared for the federal interview format, the Behavior-Based Interview, also known as the Performance-Based Interview. Be prepared to give examples in answers to seven to ten questions that will be situation or experience based. If you have an example of how you led a team, provided training, or managed a project, be prepared to talk about the project and teamwork. The best answers will be examples that demonstrate your past performance.

Know the Paperwork

Know the vacancy announcement, agency mission, and office function. Read your resume and KSAs out loud with enthusiasm. Become convinced that you are very well qualified for the job and that the agency NEEDS you to help achieve their mission.

Do Your Research

Go online to research the agency, department, and position. Read press releases about the organization. Go to www.washingtonpost.com and search for the organization to see if there are any recent news events.

Confidence, Knowledge, and Skills

In order to "sell" yourself for a new position, you have to believe in your abilities. Read books and listen to tapes that will help boost your confidence and give you the support you need to "brag" on your work skills. Don't forget or be afraid to use "I"!

Practice

In front of a mirror, tape recorder, video camera, family member, friend, anyone who agrees to listen to you.

Telephone Interview

Prepare as though you are meeting the person in an office. Get dressed nicely, have your papers neatly organized, create a quiet environment, and project a focused listening and communications style. If you are great on the phone, you can get a second interview.

Individual Interview

For the one-on-one interview, get ready for an unknown Q&A format. Prepare your questions and answers ahead of time and be ready. Be friendly and professional, and answer the questions. Practice for this interview.

Group/Panel Interview

Two to six professional staff will interview you and observe your answers. This is a difficult interview format, but it is not used too often. Just look at the person asking the question while he or she is speaking. Answer the question by looking at the person asking, but look around the room as well.

Tell Me About Yourself

Write a three-minute introduction that you could use in an interview. It should include information relevant to the position.

A Significant Accomplishment

Write one significant accomplishment that you will describe in an interview.

Select Your Best Competencies

Make a list of your best core competencies.

Write Your Most Critical Skills

Make a list of your best skills that will be most marketable to this employer.

SUCCESS STORY FROM PATRICK!

Kathryn,

First, YES...your coaching was a great help. I think it is safe to say that I knocked the ball out of the ballpark with my interview. I killed it.

Creating and then rehearsing/studying my 5 achievements was extremely valuable. It made the interview a breeze. I felt comfortable and many times my answers were so complete and detailed that I answered a couple questions at one time. (I had 9 questions in total and the interview was about 55 minutes in length.

Very optimistic that I have a good shot at the job. When I told one of the interviewers at the end I had another interview next week with another division, he said "well, I'm going to have to go poison that well" - meaning they want me pretty bad. I should hear some news soon and will let you know what happens.

Thanks again, Patrick

Patrick was hired as an Emergency Management Specialist!

Typical interview questions will be:

Job-Related

Open-Ended

Behavior-Based

Skill- and Competency-Based

Competency-Based Sample Interview Questions

Often, an interviewer will ask questions that directly relate to a competency required for the position. Here are some examples.

Attention to Detail: Describe a project you were working on that required attention to detail.

Communication: Describe a time when you had to communicate under difficult circumstances.

Conflict Management: Describe a situation where you found yourself working with someone who didn't like you. How did you handle it?

Continuous Learning: Describe a time when you recognized a problem as an opportunity.

Customer Service: Describe a situation in which you demonstrated an effective customer service skill.

Decisiveness: Tell me about a time when you had to stand up for a decision you made even though it made you unpopular.

Leadership: Describe a time when you exhibited participatory management.

Planning, Organizing, Goal Setting: Describe a time when you had to complete multiple tasks. What method did you use to manage your time?

Presentation: Tell me about a time when you developed a lesson, training, or briefing and presented it to a group.

Problem Solving: Describe a time when you analyzed data to determine multiple solutions to a problem. What steps did you take?

Resource Management: Describe a situation when you capitalized on an employee's skill.

Team Work: Describe a time when you had to deal with a team member who was not pulling his/her weight.

Present your best competencies with a great story or example that demonstrates your real behavior.

LEADERSHIP – Inspires, motivates, and guides others toward strategic/operation goals and corporate values. Coaches, mentors, and challenges staff and adapts leadership style to various situations. Consistently demonstrates decisiveness in day-to-day actions. Takes unpopular positions when necessary. Faces adversity head on. Rallies support and strives for consensus to accomplish tasks. Leads by personal example. Demonstrates concern for employees' welfare and safety, by continuously monitoring and eliminating potentially hazardous or unhealthy work situations.

Can you give me an example where you led a team?

CONTEXT:

CHALLENGE:

ACTION:

1.

2.

3.

RESULTS:

Prep for your interview using our free CCAR Accomplishment Builder!
www.resume-place.com/resources/ccar-builder/

Negotiating Your Job Offer

CONGRATULATIONS—YOU RECEIVED YOUR JOB OFFER!

Sample job offer

Congratulations! You have been tentatively selected for a position as a Social Worker GS-0185-11 located at Fort Hood, TX.

The starting salary for this position is set at GS-0185-11 (Step 1, $59,246) per annum, which includes a locality payment of 14.35%.

Now what? You can now negotiate the offer with a Superior Qualifications Justification Narrative!

Superior Qualifications Determination

An agency may determine that a candidate has superior qualifications based on—

- the level, type, or quality of the candidate's skills or competencies demonstrated or obtained through experience and/or education;
- the quality of the candidate's accomplishments compared to others in the field; or
- other factors that support a superior qualifications determination.

The candidate's skills, competencies, experience, education, and/or accomplishments must be relevant to the requirements of the position to be filled. These qualities must be significantly higher than that needed to be minimally qualified for the position and/or be of a more specialized quality compared to other candidates.

https://www.opm.gov/policy-data-oversight/pay-leave/pay-administration/fact-sheets/superior-qualifications-and-special-needs-pay-setting-authority/

Key negotiation points:

- Request for a day or two to evaluate and respond to the offer.
- The job offer will not be withdrawn in response to your negotiation request.
- Prepare a written statement to make your request and explain your justification. Send this statement to the HR specialist, who will present the document to the hiring manager for consideration if needed.
- Your chances of success with negotiation will depend on many variables, such as your qualifications, the organization budget, and the importance of the position to the organization mission.
- In some situations, if you reject the job offer, the agency will need to restart the hiring process again to fill the position. At other times, there will be a list of candidates ranked in order for hiring, and the next applicant will be offered the position if you reject it.

What can you negotiate?

- Salary
- Annual leave
- Recruitment incentive
- Telework

- Tuition reimbursement
- Reasonable accommodations
- Relocation expenses
- Commuter transit subsidy

Salary

You must accept the grade level that was advertised in the announcement, but you can negotiate your step within the grade level, all the way up to Step 10. To negotiate a higher grade, write a Superior Qualifications letter or memo to explain why your qualifications are significantly higher than what is required for the position or others who have applied. You can include salary information if it is greater than their offer.

Annual Leave

Did you know? Your non-federal work experience may also be considered towards the calculation of your annual leave if it will serve to achieve an agency mission or performance goal.

More details: www.globalsecurity.org/military/library/report/crs/crs_rl31518.pdf

Recruitment Incentive

Some agencies may have a plan in place to pay a recruitment incentive if the position is difficult to fill.

www.opm.gov/policy-data-oversight/pay-leave/recruitment-relocation-retention-incentives/fact-sheets/recruitment-incentives/

Telework

You can ask if your position qualifies for part-time telecommuting.

www.telework.gov/guidance-legislation/telework-guidance/recruitment-retention/

Tuition Reimbursement

If you or your children have federal student loans, you can ask for the organization to assist with your student loan repayment before you accept the position.

www.opm.gov/policy-data-oversight/pay-leave/student-loan-repayment/

Reasonable Accommodations

If you are a Schedule A applicant, you can ask for reasonable accommodations to help you perform your job, such as modifications to facilities for accessibility, modification of work schedule or location, and/or equipment. www.telework.gov/guidance-legislation/telework-guidance/reasonable-accommodations/

Relocation Expenses

Many vacancy announcements will state that moving expenses will not be reimbursed. However, if you have leverage in the negotiation process, and you do have to move, you could ask for some compensation toward your moving expenses.

The results of offer negotiation vary widely and depend on the agency, the budget, your qualifications, your narrative request, and the supervisor's decision. What we tell people is that it will not hurt you to ask.

Possible Responses from HR

- If your request is accepted, congratulations on your new position!
- If your request is partially accepted and a revised offer is extended to you, you can accept or reject that offer, or present a counter offer.
- When the hiring agency is no longer willing to make any more adjustments to the offer, then you will need to decide whether or not to accept the position.

Dear Rachel Downing,

Congratulations! You have been tentatively selected for a position as a Social Worker GS-0185-11 located at Fort Hood, TX.

The starting salary for this position is set at GS-0185-11(Step 10, $77,019) per annum, which includes a locality payment of 14.35%. Federal employees are paid every other Thursday, by direct deposit.

Your Federal benefits include the following: Annual and Sick Leave, Thrift Savings Plan (TSP), yearly cost of living increases, and periodic base pay increases. You are also eligible to participate in: Health, Life, Dental and Vision Insurance; Flexible Spending Account.

To learn more about federal benefits and entitlements, you can visit the following websites.

http://www.abc.army.mil/ or http://www.opm.gov/index.asp.
https://www.opm.gov/healthcare-insurance/healthcare/enrollment/new-federal-employee-enrollment/
https://www.opm.gov/healthcare-insurance/life-insurance/enrollment/
https://www.benefeds.com/Portal/
EducationSupport?EnsSubmit=EducationSupportMainCnt&ctoken=jjrWLeCx
https://www.tsp.gov/PlanParticipation/EligibilityAndContributions/establishingAccount.html
https://www.opm.gov/healthcare-insurance/flexible-spending-accounts/

This offer will remain tentative until you are able to meet the condition(s) of employment listed below.

- This position requires the incumbent to consent to criminal history background checks for employees in Child Care Services.
- This position has a mandatory seasonal influenza vaccination requirement.

PLEASE DO NOT LEAVE YOUR JOB OR GIVE NOTICE TO YOUR PRESENT EMPLOYER AT THIS TIME. THIS TENTATIVE OFFER CAN BE WITHDRAWN AT ANY TIME PRIOR TO ENTRANCE ON DUTY (EOD).

Please reply with your acceptance/declination of this tentative job offer within 2 business days, 7-Nov-2016. If you are accepting this tentative job offer, please complete the attached OF-306 and return via the SAFE website.

RESULT: Unfortunately, this job was rescinded due to budget cuts.
Very disappointing, but this can happen!

To: John Mercens, Human Resources, Center for Disease Control and Prevention

From: Carlisle Amhearst

Subject: Superior Qualifications Statement for Training Specialist (GS-12)

Date: February 2, 20xx

Thank you for the offer of employment for the Training Specialist position with the Center for Disease Control and Prevention's Office of Public Health Preparedness and Response. I look forward to having the opportunity to contribute to the development and implementation of training to support the mission of the Division of State and Local Readiness.

At this time, I would like to request that based upon superior qualifications, I receive an increase to GS-12 Step 4 or a sign-on bonus in the amount of 25% of my starting pay.

Through my education and work experience, I have had the opportunity to demonstrate superior qualifications in the following ways:

1. I have planned, directed, and taught a variety of public health preparedness and emergency response courses over the past five years for the Maryland Fire and Rescue Institute and the past three years for Howard Community College, totaling to over 25 courses taught.

2. I have prepared a wide array of teaching materials for and taught over 30 public health science courses over the past nine years at the University of Maryland.

3. My doctoral dissertation research has directly prepared me to focus on assessment and learning outcomes.

4. My educational background includes doctoral training in Biomedical Sciences Education, a Masters degree in Infectious Disease Education, and a Bachelors degree in Cell and Molecular Biology and Genetics.

5. I have served on the front lines in emergency response for the past fifteen years as an Emergency Medical Technician and Firefighter with the Laurel and Beltsville Volunteer Fire Departments in Prince George's County, Maryland, just outside of Washington, DC.

I sincerely appreciate your consideration of this request, and I look forward to beginning a rewarding career with the Centers for Disease Control and Prevention and making an impact within the Office of Public Health Preparedness and Response.

RESULT: SUCCESS!

The offer was changed to GS 12, Step 4 from the original offer of Step 1.

Index

1. Founder, President, and Manager of The Resume Place®, the first federal job search consulting and federal resume writing service in the world, and the producer of www.resume-place.com, the first website devoted to federal resume writing.

2. Pioneer designer of the federal resume format in 1995 with the publication of the leading resource for federal human resources and jobseekers worldwide—the *Federal Resume Guidebook*, now in its sixth edition.

3. Developer of the Ten Steps to a Federal Job®, a licensed curriculum and turnkey training program taught by more than 2,000 Certified Federal Job Search Trainers™ (CFJST) around the world.

4. Leading Federal Resume Writing, KSA, Resumix, ECQ and Federal Interview government contracted trainer. GSA Schedule Holder.

5. Author of numerous federal career publications (in addition to the *Federal Resume Guidebook* mentioned above):

The *Military to Federal Career Guide* is the first book for military personnel and is now in its second edition, featuring veteran federal resumes. Troutman recognized the need for returning military personnel from Iraq, Afghanistan, and Kosovo to have a resource available to them in their searches for government jobs.

Ten Steps to a Federal Job was published two months after 9/11 and was written for private industry jobseekers seeking first-time positions in the federal government, where they could contribute to our nation's security. Now in its third edition.

The *Jobseeker's Guide* started initially as the companion course handout to the *Ten Steps* book, but captured its own following when it became the handout text used by over 200 military installations throughout the world for transitioning military and family members. Now in its eighth edition.

With the looming human capital crisis and baby boomers retiring in government, the *Student's Federal Career Guide* was co-authored with Kathryn's daughter and MPP graduate, Emily Troutman, and is the first book for students pursuing a federal job. Now in its third edition, including the latest information on the changing structure of student programs, plus additional guidance for veterans taking advantage of the Post-9/11 GI Bill.

Resumes for Dummies by Joyce Lain Kennedy is renowned as the premier guidebook for resume writing. Kathryn and The Resume Place staff served as designers and producers of all the private industry resume samples for the fifth edition.

Charles Clark
Federal Human Resources Consultant

Charles Clark is a Federal Human Resources Specialist with a broad background in Diversity and Inclusion Programs, Veterans Employment Programs, Schedule A Hiring of Individuals with Disabilities, and Reasonable Accommodations for individuals with disabilities. Charles has received numerous accolades and recognition for training federal hiring managers, college career counselors, and military transition counselors on the federal staffing process so they can better assist veterans and individuals with disabilities seeking federal employment.

Charles began his federal career following a 24-year military career with the U.S. Air Force, culminating as the Superintendent of the Air Force District of Washington's Manpower, Personnel and Service Directorate (A1). As the AFDW/A1 Superintendent, he oversaw a 120-person headquarters staff responsible for managing 350+ human resources programs for the command's 40,000 military and civilian employees around the world. Prior assignments included serving as the Department of Defense's Presidential Support Program Manager, responsible for staffing high-level sensitive military vacancies at the White House and other high-priority vacancies at the Pentagon; Senior Enlisted Advisor to the Executive Secretary for the Department of Defense; and HR Superintendent for the Air Force's Office of Special Investigations (OSI).

Charles' keen knowledge of federal staffing procedures, coupled with his vast experience with non-competitive hiring authorities for veterans, disabled veterans, and individuals with disabilities, has proven extremely successful in the hiring of individuals from these targeted groups into positions throughout the federal government.

Paulina Chen
Developmental Editor & Interior Page Layout

Paulina was working at the U.S. Environmental Protection Agency when Kathryn came to the EPA to provide federal resume consultations. Kathryn noticed Paulina's ability to communicate complex information in a straightforward, easy-to-understand way. Kathryn offered Paulina her first freelance opportunity—to design and lay out the interior pages for the first edition of *Ten Steps to a Federal Job*. Now many years later, this team is still producing award-winning and best-selling books. As mentioned in the introduction, Paulina is returning to government, but she hopes to continue collaborating with Kathryn Troutman and The Resume Place on these ground-breaking publications.

Military Transition to Federal Career Services: Consulting and Expert Writing

Whether you are staying the same field of work from the military, or changing careers, the Certified Federal Resume Writers at The Resume Place, Inc., can write a targeted, expert Best qualified federal resume for you. We write the resumes in the Outline Format with Keywords and Accomplishments.

We are pleased to offer America's veterans the following:

- Veteran career consultation, full service federal resumes, and cover letters

The Resume Place Resume writers and editors follow the Ten Steps to a Federal Job® techniques as written in this book. Our expert writers will:

- Discuss your federal career objectives and specialized experience
- Recommend the best occupational series for you based on experience
- Analyze and translate your military experience into the federal writing style and terminology that the federal human resources specialists will require
- Coach you in the best accomplishments to demonstrate your expertise and knowledge for the new target position
- Write the duties and responsibilities to match the keywords in the target announcement
- Write the keywords IN ALL CAPS for the HR reviewers (the USAJOBs system is a HUMAN resume reading system – not automated)
- Edit the resume and ensure that the positions will stand out that will demonstrate your Specialized Experience

Get help applying for federal jobs with USAJOBS:

We will ensure that your USAJOBS account is correct, documents are uploaded and your resume is successfully in the builder. Our USAJOBS support and advisory services help you apply for positions correctly.

Check out these useful websites:

- *Free Federal Resume Builder, KSA Builder, Cover Letter Builder and Application Writing Builders* www.resume-place.com/resources
- vetfedjobs.org
- www.fedshirevets.gov
- *Mil2FedJobs:* www.dllr.state.md.us/mil2fedjobs

All RP Military Transition Federal Resume Writers are Certified Federal Job Search Trainers/ Certified Federal Resume Writers

The Resume Place, Inc.
www.resume-place.com
888-480-8265

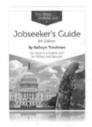  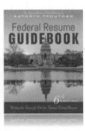    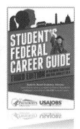

Order online at www.fedjobtraining.com | Bulk Orders: (888) 480 8265
FREE SHIPPING of bulk orders in the domestic US and APO; shipping is calculated for HI and overseas

EBooks Available for Immediate Download
Many of our titles are available in PDF or Kindle versions for immediate download when ordered from our site.

Jobseeker's Guide, 8th Edition
Military to Federal Career Transition Resource Workbook and guide for the Ten Steps to a Federal Job® training curriculum. Federal job search strategies for first-time jobseekers who are separating military and family members. *$18.95 ea., Bulk Rates Available*

The Stars Are Lined Up for Military Spouses
Federal Jobs for Mliitary Spouses through USAJOBS, Program S, NAF and Excepted Service
Key book to assist military spouses with navigating the complex federal job process. Covers four ways to land the major kinds of federal positions for military spouses. *$14.95 ea., Bulk Rates Available*

Federal Resume Guidebook, 6th Ed.
Now the #2 Resume Book in America! The ultimate guide in federal resume and KSA writing. Easy to use as a template for writing. Specialty occupational series chapters. *$15.95 ea., Bulk Rates Available*

The New SES Application, 2nd Ed.
The SES job application is complex. The New SES Application breaks it down into a step-by-step process based on a popular workshop taught for over 10 years. Plus, the book has updated the SES info to help you navigate hiring reforms currently impacting the Senior Executive Service. *$21.95 ea., Bulk Rates Available*

Student's Federal Career Guide, 3rd Ed.
3rd Edition takes the 2013 IndieFab Gold Winner for Career Books! Outstanding book for jobseekers who are just getting out of college and whose education will help the applicant get qualified for a position. 20 samples of recent graduate resumes with emphasis on college degrees, courses, major papers, internships, and relevant work experiences. Outstanding usability of samples on the CD-ROM. *$9.95 ea., print copies sold out; available in PDF*

Creating Your First Resume
Creating Your First Resume is a book that will be used at high school and technical school programs nationwide. The new edition boasts brand new resume samples that represent the push toward STEM technical programs to provide training and certifications for high school students. *$12.95 ea., Bulk Rates Available*

Ten Steps to a Federal Job, 3rd Ed.
Written for a first-time applicant, particularly those making a career change from private industry to federal government. Case studies include 24 before & after successful resumes! *$18.95 ea., Bulk Rates Available*

Online Federal Resume Database
This Online Federal Resume Database contains more than 110 resume samples and federal job search resources from the current Resume Place publications. Each CD-ROM has a clearly organized interface. Sample resumes are available in Word and PDF format for quick previewing and easy editing. *Individual and Agency / Base Licenses Available*

Train-the-Trainer Federal Career Certification in Ten Steps to a Fedral Job®

Since 1992, over 2,000 career professionals have benefited from our unique certification in the Ten Steps to a Federal Job® curriculum, and the program continues to grow each year. Get certified and licensed to teach Kathryn Troutman's popular, proven, turnkey curriculum: Ten Steps to a Federal Job® and Federal Resume & KSA Writing curriculum. This course was developed by Kathryn Troutman as a direct result of her training experiences at hundreds of federal agencies throughout the world.

Teach Ten Steps at your military transition center, career center or workforce center. Our curriculum is easy to teach, friendly, and results in more jobseekers applying successfully for federal positions.

Registration Benefits - Incredible Value!

Three year license to access valuable training tools and online resources and to be able to teach our Ten Steps curriculum

Federal Career Books for Your Library:

- ❏ *Federal Resume Guidebook*
- ❏ *Jobseeker's Guide*
- ❏ *Student's Federal Career Guide*
- ❏ *Creating Your First Resume*
- ❏ *The New SES Application*
- ❏ *The Stars Are Lined Up for Military Spouses*

PowerPoint Presentations for your use as a trainer:

- ◊ Ten Steps to a Federal Job®
- ◊ The Stars Are Lined Up for Military Spouses with PPP-S
- ◊ USAJOBS Navigation
- ◊ Ten Steps to a Pathways Internship for Students and Recent Grads

"I just wanted to let you know that attendance at the three-day course in March has done wonders for my confidence and wonders for my clients. When we go through the OPM Job Factors and the Grading of GS positions, most clients are over-joyed to have opened the "treasure chest" where the mystery of pursuing a Federal Job Position is solved. Thank you for all that you do!! I love the books and find something new EVERY day that I can share with my fellow coaches."

More Information and Registration

www.fedjobtraining.com/certification-programs.htm